Veiled
IN BEAUTY

CREATIVE PUBLISHING international

CHANHASSEN, MINNESOTA
www.creativepub.com

President/CEO: Michael Eleftheriou
Vice President/Publisher: Linda Ball
Vice President/Retail Sales: Kevin Haas

VEILED IN BEAUTY
Created by: The Editors of Creative Publishing international, Inc.

Executive Editor: Elaine Perry
Managing Editor: Yen Le
Senior Editor: Linda Neubauer
Art Director: Megan Noller
Project & Photo Stylist: Joanne Wawra
Samplemakers: Arlene Dohrman, Teresa Henn
Researcher: Joan Bakken
Prop Stylist: Christine Jahns
Photographer: Andrea Rugg
Director of Production Services: Kim Gerber
Production Manager: Stasia Dorn
Contributors: Beacon Adhesives; C.M. Offray & Sons, Inc.;
Duncan Enterprises; Judith M. Hat & Millinery Supplies;
Milliners Supply Company; University Products

Copyright © 2001 Stockbyte photographs on pages
1, 4/5, 6, 24/25, 54, 73, and Back cover

ISBN 1-58923-047-7

Printed on American paper by:
R. R. Donnelley
10 9 8 7 6 5 4 3 2 1

Creative Publishing international, Inc. offers a variety of
how-to books. For information write:
    Creative Publishing international, Inc.
        Subscriber Books
    18705 Lake Drive East
    Chanhassen, Minnesota 55317

Contents

Introduction

YOU'VE set the date, now it's time to
set the wedding-preparation wheels in motion.
The excitement and anticipation builds
as all your efforts are made to further your
ultimate goal—to make your wedding day
the most beautiful day of your life. You
have taken a step in the right direction by
choosing to handcraft some of the important
elements. Your personally designed headpiece
and veil will far surpass a comparable
ready-to-wear set in quality and panache.
Because they are handmade originals, not
cookie-cutter replicas worn by hundreds
of other brides, you will wear them with pride
and treasure them for a lifetime.

Choosing a Style

*I*MAGES of the perfect wedding, like the brides who envision

them, come in every style imaginable. Some brides may adhere strictly to

traditional attire and ceremony, while others feel more comfortable

in casual or unconventional settings. One tradition almost every bride

keeps is to wear something on her head. Born of ancient rituals

concerned with shielding the betrothed from evil or guaranteeing her

virginity, the headpiece and veil have evolved today into a fashion

statement that symbolizes the bride's sisterhood with all other brides

before her. What she wears on her head, whether it is a scattering of

jeweled hair picks, a wreath of fresh flowers, or a lace-covered

Juliet cap and veil, signifies her bridal stature on her wedding day.

The first rule for designing head attire is that it must complement the dress; be consistent with its direction (traditional, contemporary, or period) and style (ultraformal, informal, or somewhere in between). Its real purpose is to bring the focal point of the ensemble to the bride's face, flattering her in every way. The elements for constructing the headpiece and veil come in a wide range of options, so for every bride there are several possibilities that fulfill both requirements beautifully.

1

2

5

Fabrics & Nets

FABRIC used on the headpiece or for a bias bound edge finish (page 82) on a veil should match the gown in color and be similar in style. If fabric remnants left over from the gown construction or alterations are not available to you, visit the fabric store for samples of fabric options. Compare the samples to the gown in natural light; there are many shades of white and off-white in the bridal department. Popular bridal fabrics include a variety of SATINS (1), which have a shiny surface. Even if the gown is made of a heavy satin, a lighter weight satin can be used for the headpiece. SILK SHANTUNG (2), very pliable and easy to work with, is lightweight with fine filaments and slubs throughout. DOUPPIONI SILK (3) has firm body and lustrous sheen, characterized by irregular slubs throughout the fabric. There are synthetic fabrics that imitate silks, but may not be as easy to work with or match in color. TAFFETA (4) has a crisp hand and drapes stiffly. It is characterized by the rustling sound that occurs when layers are brushed together. BROCADES (5) have raised floral or figured patterns that stand out against twill or satin backgrounds. It may be difficult to find a brocade that matches the gown, but a smaller-scale brocade in the same color would work very well for a coordinating headpiece.

3

4

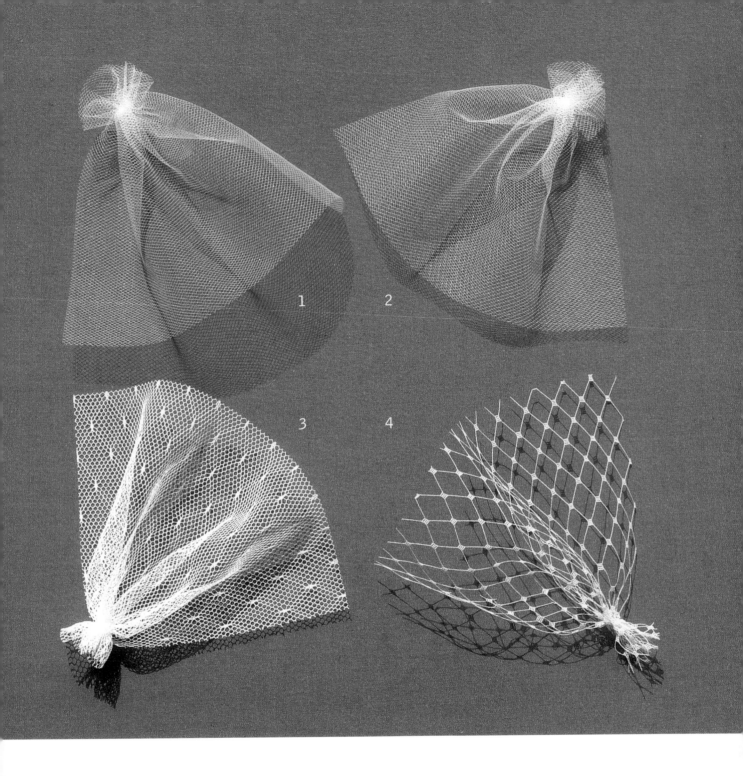

NYLON ILLUSION (1), a fine, delicate mesh that is soft and drapable, is the most commonly used netting for veils. It is available in widths of 72", 108", and 144" (183, 274.5, and 366 cm), in a variety of whites: white, diamond white, eggshell, blush, and ivory, in a plain or sparkle finish. The subtle differences in color are more apparent when the illusion is gathered up or layered. TULLE (2) is slightly heavier than illusion and comes in a variety of colors, usually 54" (137 cm) wide. POINT D'ESPRIT (3) is a coarser netting with a dotted design. RUSSIAN (OR FRENCH) VEILING (4) is a stiff, dramatic, diamond-shaped mesh, useful for face veils or as accents on headpieces and hats.

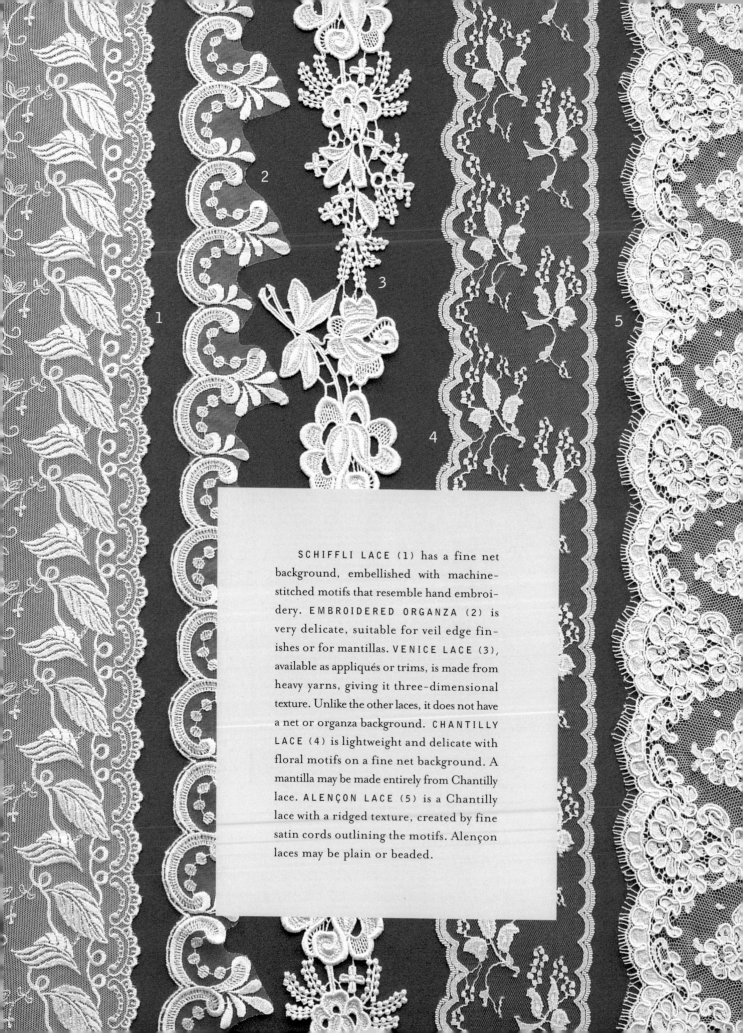

SCHIFFLI LACE (1) has a fine net background, embellished with machine-stitched motifs that resemble hand embroidery. EMBROIDERED ORGANZA (2) is very delicate, suitable for veil edge finishes or for mantillas. VENICE LACE (3), available as appliqués or trims, is made from heavy yarns, giving it three-dimensional texture. Unlike the other laces, it does not have a net or organza background. CHANTILLY LACE (4) is lightweight and delicate with floral motifs on a fine net background. A mantilla may be made entirely from Chantilly lace. ALENÇON LACE (5) is a Chantilly lace with a ridged texture, created by fine satin cords outlining the motifs. Alençon laces may be plain or beaded.

Laces & Trims

LACE styles are very distinctive and are often named after the European area where they were first made. The lace used on a veil or headpiece does not have to match the gown lace, but for consistency, it should be the same style. Laces can be found as wide fabrics, narrow trims, or as individual appliqués. Individual motifs can be cut from some fabric laces and wide trims to be appliquéd on the veil or glued to the headpiece. Lace edgings are often used on veil edges, the underside of the headpiece, or on narrow headpieces, like bun wraps, crowns, or headbands.

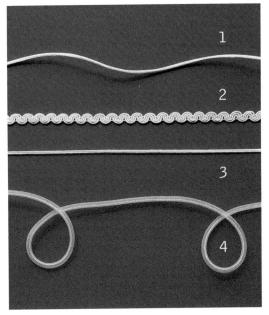

GALLOON LACE TRIMS (1) have identical patterns on both sides, facing away from each other. Most galloons can be used as a wide trim or cut apart down the center so each edge can be used separately. **EDGINGS (2)** are narrow trims with one decorative edge and one straight edge. Widths range from 1/4" to 6" (6 mm to 15 cm). **LACE APPLIQUÉS (3)** are individual motifs, often available in mirror-image pairs, which makes them especially desirable for symmetrical headpieces or as embellishments on a veil.

RATTAIL (1) is a satin-covered cording that can be used for veil edge finishes or attached to headpieces in soft loops and curves. **GIMP (2)** is a decorative braid made of fine cording, used for defining the outer edge of a headpiece or for covering raw fabric edges on the underside. **SOUTACHE BRAID (3)** has two fine cords wrapped tightly together side by side, leaving a groove between them for stitching. Stiff and flexible, **HORSEHAIR TUBING (4)** can be used for decorative loop accents or for covering bare millinery wires.

CRESCENTS OR BANDEAUS

These slightly curved bands come in various shapes and sizes. They can be worn flat on top of the head, tipped up in front of an upswept hairdo, or in the back of the head below an updo. The oblong crescent, at left, is covered with satin brocade and adorned with handmade ribbon flowers. The two-tier veil with a pouf is accented with a ribbon edge finish.

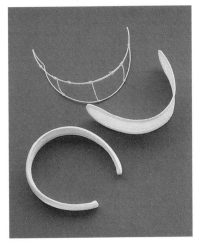

HEADBANDS *Worn on top of the head with long or short hair, a headband can be understated, with a simple silk ribbon embroidery design, or more elaborate, perhaps with flowers, lace, or pearls. Almost any style of veil will work well, including the bouffant veil with machine-stitched scallops, shown here. A headband is a good choice for attaching a cascade or full-circle veil, when the upper layer will be worn as a blusher.*

CROWNS & BUN WRAPS

Circular headpieces of uniform height have a formal appearance. Because they are decorated completely around, they are usually worn encircling an upswept hairdo. Small-diameter crowns, referred to as bun wraps, seemingly hold the hair in controlled curls at the top of the head. This elegant bun wrap is embellished with serpentine-gathered ribbon and a twisted strand of pearls. The single veil, edged with pearls, is attached to a large comb for easy removal after the ceremony. Another option is to simply attach a short veil under the back edge of the bun wrap. For larger-diameter crowns, the veil can be attached to the back side of the crown front, covering the hair and crown in a sheer cloud. Or it can be attached to the inside back of the crown, either from the top or bottom, depending on the look you prefer.

TIARAS *Similar to crowns, tiaras are higher in front, narrowing as they wrap to the sides. They are often open in the back, or have a thin support wire for attaching the veil or to be hidden under the hair. Classic buckram tiaras are covered with bead-encrusted lace; a more sheer version may feature pearls glued in open designs over horsehair braid. A popular contemporary choice is a tiara made of rhinestones, wired crystals, or wired pearls. This two-tier ripple-edge veil is attached to the back support wire. Other veil options include a bouffant veil attached behind the tiara front or a modest pouf attached to the back.*

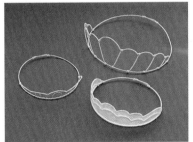

V-BANDS *Encircling the top of the head and coming to a point at the forehead, a V-band headpiece can be a stunning choice. As if pointing to the main attraction, the V-band draws all eyes to the bride's face. Some styles are merely a wire covered with pearls or rhinestones. Others, like the one shown here, are wire forms covered with buckram or horsehair, adorned with lace motifs or small silk flowers. Hair can be worn upswept inside the headpiece or down, with the veil attached at the back. This headpiece style also works very well with a flattering pouf at the back.*

WREATHS *An informal floral wreath is a fitting choice for an outdoor venue or simply because the bride loves flowers. Fresh or artificial blooms are secured to a wire form, created to fit the bride perfectly. Clustering large flowers at the back helps control the widening effect that wreaths can have. A veil secured to a comb is easily removed for dancing. At left, ribbon streamers, attached to a silk flower wreath offer a more casual look.*

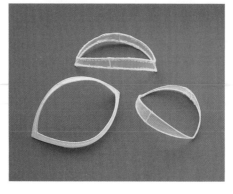

BENT BANDS *This headpiece shape begins as a circle that is bent on opposite sides and shaped to fit the head. It offers more fullness at the sides, flattering for a bride with a narrow face. Hair can be worn in an upsweep inside the opening when both bands are decorative. Then the veil is attached under the lower edge of the back band, like the full-circle veil shown here. Sometimes the back band is merely a bare support wire, which can be hidden under hair that is worn down, making it suitable for shorter hair styles. A veil can then be attached under the back edge of the front band. A plain back band can also be worn over the hair and used for attaching the veil.*

JULIET CAPS *A close-fitting headpiece that sits back on top of the head, the Juliet cap can be worn with various hairstyles. It is a good choice for brides with short or fine hair, as it fits snugly and feels secure; some styles even have an extra support wire in the back. Tall brides favor Juliet caps because they don't add height. Veils of all styles and lengths, with or without poufs, work well with Juliet caps. The deep scallop-cut veil edge, accented with pearls and sequins, echoes the swirls of lace on the headpiece below.*

TEARDROPS *A teardrop form is actually a small hat with a point at the front, directing all eyes toward the bride's happy face. This is another favorite for brides who don't want to add height, though it is equally attractive with a stylish pouf at the back. More height and emphasis can be added with a raised cluster of ribbon roses. In the version below, the form is covered with ivory satin and a delicately embroidered lace. The upper layer of the bias bound cascade veil is worn forward as a blusher for the trip to the altar.*

HATS *There are many styles and sizes of bridal hat forms from which to choose. Bare horsehair or buckram forms can be embellished with lace, ribbons, netting, or fabric, depending on the bride's mood and preferences. Some hats are partially adorned with satin or other fabric and may need only the addition of a bow or a cluster of ribbon flowers to make them complete. Wide brimmed hats usually have support wires stitched into the outer edges or are stiffened with buckram to keep the brims from flopping forward. A tube pouf and short half-circle veil of point d'esprit add a bridal touch to the horsehair picture hat above. A braided gimp trim covers the support wire while defining the outer edge of the brim.*

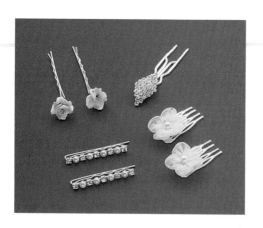

SMALL HAIR ACCESSORIES

Short metal combs adorned with wired crystals enhance an upswept hairdo for a semiformal look. The shimmer of the crystals is repeated in the fine iridescent cord applied to the edge of the elbow-length, separately attached veil. Barrettes, banana clips, and large bobby pins also can be decked out with sparkling pearls, rhinestones, and beads to bring the eyes of the beholders to the bride's face.

MANTILLAS *Inspired by Spanish tradition, a mantilla is a lace-edged circle of netting or lace fabric. The circle can be any diameter from 36" to 108" (91.5 to 274.5 cm), bearing in mind that the larger the circle, the more weight the attachment points must bare. A mantilla can be secured to the hair via a hidden comb attached under wide lace edging in front. For the all-over lace mantilla above, individual elastic button loops were discreetly secured to the underside of several embroidered flowers, providing attachment with bobby pins.*

Designing a Headpiece

t **H E** perfect headpiece coordinates beautifully with the wedding gown, but that doesn't mean that the headpiece and veil designed by the dress manufacturer are perfect for the bride who buys the dress. The headpiece should be designed to enhance the bride's bone structure and facial proportions, to highlight her best features and camouflage her flaws. Because many brides choose to remove the veil after the ceremony, the headpiece should be designed first and feel complete without the veil. Ultimately, the perfect headpiece reflects the bride's personality, and she feels at ease wearing it.

Two things must be done before designing the headpiece: select the gown and decide on a hairstyle. Take a picture or sketch of the dress to your hairstylist long before the wedding and seek advice on the best hairstyle and headpiece style to complement your face and the dress. If possible, cut a T-shirt to resemble the dress neckline, and wear it for the brainstorming session. Select a hairstyle that you are comfortable wearing; don't make any severe changes just for the wedding. You will want to be able to recognize yourself in your wedding pictures!

To make the headpiece work to your advantage, keep these general guidelines in mind. Consider your face shape. If you are the perfect oval, almost any style headpiece will work for you. If your face is wide, square, or round, select a style that will elongate your face, such as a V-band, bun wrap, narrow crescent, or tiara. Avoid full, wide circles, such as a wreath or crown; also avoid bent bands and headbands, keeping ornamentation mostly on the top of the head.

If your face is long and narrow, the shapes avoided by round-faced brides would work best for you; avoid tiaras, bun wraps, and V-bands, and go for a style that will widen your image, such as a crown, wreath, or bent band. Floral sprays at your temples, perhaps attached to the sides of a headband or Juliet cap will flatter your face.

Consider the wedding theme and venue. Some headpieces are naturally more formal than others; tiaras and crowns are more formal than wreaths or headbands. But almost any headpiece can be made to look more formal or casual with the right application of fabrics, laces, and embellishments.

Supplies for Making Headpieces

HEADPIECE forms, in many styles, are available in the bridal department of fabric stores or from mail order or Internet sources (page 96). The gallery of headpiece styles on pages 12 to 23 will help you decide which style to buy. Don't be concerned if the form feels too large for your head, as most of them are easily made smaller using WIRE CUTTERS (1) and WIRE JOINERS (2) or JEWELRY WIRE (3). To provide a base for the embellishments, wire frame headpieces are first covered with HORSEHAIR BRAID (4), available in 3" and 6" (7.5 and 15 cm) widths. The braid has a gathering cord along one edge to help shape the horsehair over the form. WHITE or IVORY COTTON FLANNEL or THIN BATTING (5) provides a bumper between the form and the outer fabric, giving the headpiece a smooth, slightly padded look. Headpieces can be covered with fabric and lace left over after sewing the gown. If you purchased the gown, ask for any discarded fabric from the alterations or look for similar fabric and lace in the fabric store. LACE MOTIFS or LACE APPLIQUÉS (6), SEQUINS, BEADS, and PEARLS (7) are secured to the covered frames with glue. PEARL or CRYSTAL MONOFILAMENT SPRAYS (8), SILK FLOWER SPRAYS and FALLS (9), WIRED NET EMBELLISHMENTS (10), or individual RIBBON or SILK FLOWERS (11) can be hand-stitched or glued in place. ELASTIC BUTTON LOOPING (12) is used to secure PLASTIC or METAL COMBS (13) and bobby pins.

There are several SPECIALIZED ADHESIVES (14) helpful for making bridal headpieces. Spray adhesive is handy for adhering the flannel or batting to the form. Fabric glues and gem glues that set up quickly and are clear and flexible when dry are the easiest to work with.

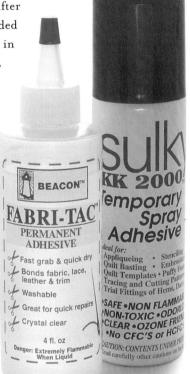

14

7

Covering a Headpiece Form

CHECK the fit of the headpiece form, wearing your hair in the general style you will be wearing on your wedding day. Some forms are simply a wire base; others are wire covered with buckram or horsehair. The form can be bent and shaped, if necessary.

Most likely, if the headpiece size needs adjusting, it needs to be made smaller, and this should be done first. Also, determine the method for attaching the headpiece. If your hair is thick or curly, a comb located at the front of the headpiece is often helpful. Many hairstylists prefer several loops placed around the outer edge for inserting bobby pins, especially if your hair is fine or straight. Clean your workspace, assemble the materials, and start designing.

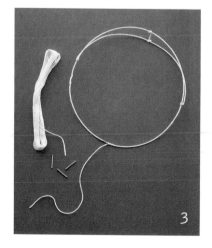

HOW TO MAKE A WIRE FORM SMALLER

1. Determine the location at which the adjustment will be made. Cut the wire(s), using a wire cutter.

2. Overlap wires the desired distance; wrap with tape, and check fit.

3. Remove tape. Wrap the overlap with jewelry wire. Or cut out the necessary section of wire, remove 1/2" (1.3 cm) thread wrap from the cut ends, and connect the ends with a wire joiner; crimp the joiner to secure. Wrap the joint with white embroidery floss or rayon thread, if it will not be covered; seal ends with glue.

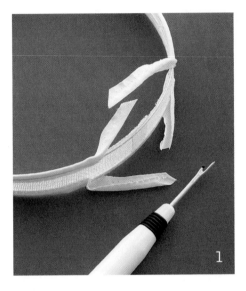

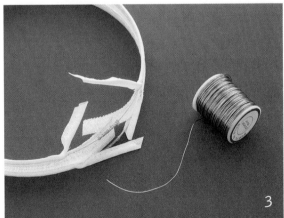

ABOVE *A wire Juliet cap form and a buckram crescent become lovely finished headpieces with a few simple steps and a little imagination.*

HOW TO MAKE A BUCKRAM FORM SMALLER

1. Determine the location at which the adjustment will be made. Remove the stitches from the bias tape that covers the outer wires at this point, about 2" (5 cm) in each direction; cut the bias tape, if necessary.

2. Cut the wires, using a wire cutter. Cut the buckram, using a scissors. Overlap the wires and buckram the desired distance; clamp with binder clips. Try on the headpiece to check fit; adjust the overlap as necessary.

3. Cut the wires at the center of the overlap and join them with a wire joiner; crimp the joiner to secure. Or wrap the overlapped wires with jewelry wire. Glue the overlapped buckram edges. Wrap the bias tape back over the wires; stitch by hand.

TIP *In altering the headpiece size, be sure to allow room for the hairstyle you will be wearing and the thickness of the veil. Veils attached with hook and loop tape need a little more room.*

HOW TO COVER A BUCKRAM FORM

1. Cut a bias piece of white flannel slightly larger than the form. Spray the wrong side of the flannel with fabric adhesive. Center the flannel over the right side of the form, and smooth it down toward the edges; trim it even with the outer edges of the form. If a more padded appearance is desired, use thin batting for this step. If the form will be heavily embellished, this step can be omitted.

2. Cut a bias piece of fabric 1" to 2" (2.5 to 5 cm) larger than the headpiece. Centering the fabric over the form, smooth the fabric down toward the edges of the headpiece; secure with pins.

3. Wrap the fabric to the inside of the headpiece, and secure with clear fabric glue, trimming and clipping the fabric, and making small tucks for a smooth fit. Allow to dry, and remove the pins.

4. Cut a piece of lace, another piece of fabric, or a length of ribbon to fit the inside surface of the form; secure with fabric glue. Glue narrow lace edging or gimp over the raw edge of lace or fabric.

5. Cut lace motifs; apply liquid fray preventer to any cut cords on lace. Arrange the lace and any additional embellishments on the headpiece as desired; secure with glue or hand stitching.

6. Apply sequins and beads or pearls, if desired; using tweezers, dip the item in glue, and secure.

7. Cut a length of button looping slightly longer than a hair comb; glue it to the inside of the frame near the front, with the loops facing the frame back. Slide the teeth of a comb into the button looping. Glue several loops of button looping at the sides of the headpiece for securing to the hair with bobby pins.

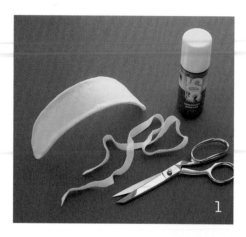

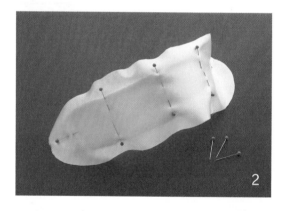

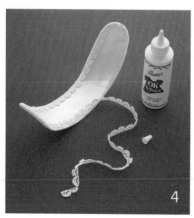

HOW TO COVER A WIRE FRAME

1. Cut wide horsehair braid 2" (5 cm) longer than
the frame. Glue the uncorded edge of the horsehair to
the widest outer edge of the frame, applying dots
of glue to the frame. Secure with plastic clothespins,
if necessary.

2. Pull on the gathering cord to shape the horsehair
to the frame. Glue the horsehair to the remaining
outer edges. Allow the glue to dry. Trim excess horsehair
even with the wire frame at the edges.

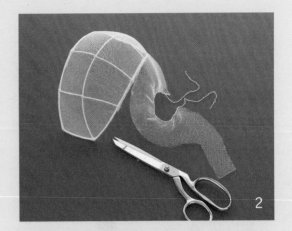

3. Follow steps 1 to 7, opposite, for covering a
buckram frame, if a fabric-covered and embellished
headpiece is desired. For a more sheer appearance,
omit steps 1 to 4, and arrange embellishments
over the horsehair, covering any wire crosspieces first
and filling in remaining areas as desired.

TIP *Arrange lace pieces to extend
off the edges of the headpiece for a softer,
more natural look. This will hide the
hard wire edges underneath while showing
off the lace against your hair.*

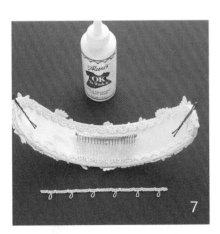

Ribbon Accents

RIBBONS, in their unlimited selection of styles and widths, are useful for creating many different accents for bridal headpieces. SATINS (1), TAFFETAS (2), JACQUARDS (3), SHEERS (4), and VELVETS (5) range in size from 1/16" to 3 1/2" (1.5 to 89 mm). Available with or without wired edges, ribbon can be gathered or pleated into interesting trims, shaped into flowers and leaves, used as loop accents for floral wreaths, or knotted and hung as streamers. Wide ribbons can be used to make beautiful bows (page 50), worn alone in the hair or at the top of a veil. When making ribbon flowers that you intend to glue or stitch onto a headpiece, hand-tack the flowers to a base of stiff, WOVEN INTERFACING (6). If the flowers will be incorporated into a wreath or arranged in cascades or falls to extend beyond the headpiece form, attach them to FLORAL WIRE (7) and wrap the stems with WHITE or GREEN FLORAL TAPE (8). Design flower centers from ARTIFICIAL STAMENS (9), pearls, sequins, crystals, or knotted ribbons.

2

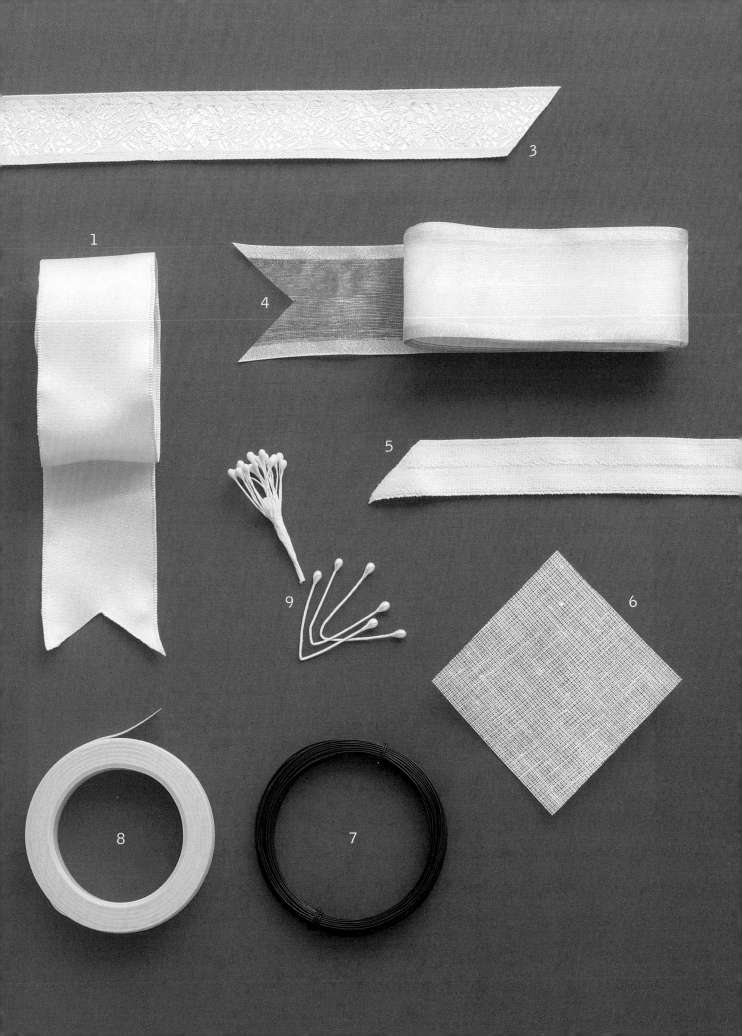

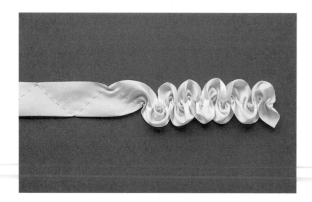

HOW TO MAKE SERPENTINE RIBBON TRIM

1. Mark off one edge of the ribbon in spaces two ribbon widths apart. Repeat on the other side, aligning the marks halfway between the marks on the opposite edge.

2. Knot the thread at the first mark. Stitch running stitches back and forth across the ribbon, wrapping the thread around the ribbon edge at each mark.

3. Gather the ribbon to the desired fullness, arranging it evenly along the thread.

HOW TO MAKE A SIMPLE RIBBON ROSETTE

1. Cut a length of ribbon equal to 5 to 15 times the ribbon width, depending on the desired fullness. Remove wire, if any, from the inner edge (the edge that will become the flower center). Apply liquid fray preventer to ends.

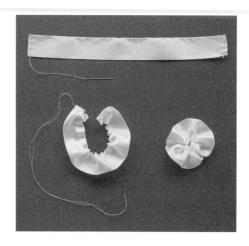

2. Thread a hand needle with double thread; knot the thread on the outer edge near one end. Stitch running stitches to the inner edge, round the corner, and stitch close to the inner edge the length of the ribbon. At the opposite end, round the corner and stitch to the outer edge.

3. Gather the ribbon tightly. Knot the end to the beginning, turning the raw edges to the flower back. Tack the flower to a small backing square of stiff, woven interfacing.

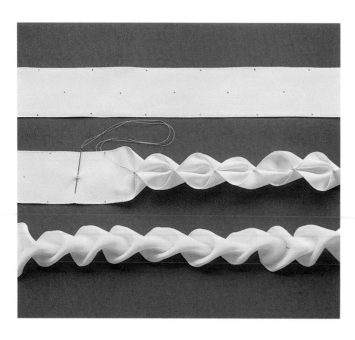

HOW TO MAKE SHELL SMOCKING RIBBON TRIM

1. Mark off both edges of the ribbon in spaces one ribbon width apart. Mark the center of the ribbon halfway between each of the outer marks. Knot thread at first outer edge mark.

2. Take a small stitch in the first center mark and another in the opposite outer mark; pull three points together and knot.

3. Knot thread at the next outer mark, allowing it to lay flat between knots.

4. Repeat steps 2 and 3 down the ribbon to the desired length.

HOW TO MAKE A FIVE-PETAL RIBBON FLOWER

1. Cut a length of ribbon equal to 12½ to 17½ times the ribbon width; remove the wire from the inner edge (the edge that will become the flower center). Apply liquid fray preventer to the ends.

2. Mark off five equal spaces along the inner edge, marking with a disappearing marking pen. Knot the thread on the inner edge near one end. Stitch running stitches in the pattern shown, wrapping the thread around the outer edge at each mark.

3. Finish the flower, following step 3, opposite.

HOW TO MAKE A LOOP RIBBON FLOWER

1. Knot the thread at one end of an 18" (46 cm) length of narrow ribbon. Take small stitches in and out of the ribbon every 2" or 3" (5 or 7.5 cm).

2. Pull up on the thread, forming loops. Knot the loops together at the base.

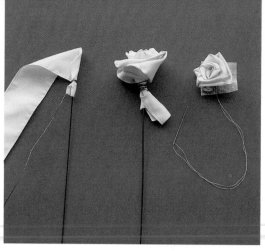

HOW TO MAKE A
WIRE RIBBON ROSE

1. Cut 16" to 32" (40.5 to 81.5 cm) of ribbon, depending on the ribbon width and desired finished size. Pull out about 2" (5 cm) of wire on one edge of one end; smooth ribbon flat. Fold 2" (5 cm) ribbon end down diagonally, then fold outer edge over. Bend a small loop in the end of a stem wire; slip the wire loop inside the ribbon folds. Wrap pulled wire around bottom of folds, forming the rose center.

2. Gather up the remaining length of ribbon tightly, sliding the ribbon along the same wire from the free end toward the rose center.

3. Wrap gathered edge around the center, wrapping each layer slightly higher than the previous one. Fold the ribbon end down and catch it under the last layer.

4. Wrap wire tightly around base to secure. Wrap floral tape around rose base, stretching tape and warming it with your fingers for best adhesion. Continue down the stem, catching ribbon leaves, opposite, as you wrap.

For a wired ribbon rose without a stem, omit the stem wire. Stitch the rose center to a backing fabric. Work the gathered ribbon around the base, tacking it in place as you go.

HOW TO MAKE
CONCERTINA ROSES

1. Cut 12" (30.5 cm) of 3/8" or 1/2" (9 or 12 mm) ribbon. Roll under diagonally at the center, forming a right angle. Turn the end that is underneath back over the center. Repeat with the other end.

2. Continue folding alternate ends back over previous folds, forming a square stack. Stop when the ends are 1" (2.5 cm) long.

3. Turn the stack over. Hold only the two ends, and release the stack. Holding ends securely but loosely enough so they can slide, pull one end gently; a rose will form. Stop pulling when the excess ribbon is pulled out and the center of the rose sinks in. Tack to a backing. Trim away the excess ribbon.

HOW TO MAKE
A TRADITIONAL
RIBBON ROSE

1. Keeping ribbon on reel, fold 2" (5 cm) ribbon end down diagonally, then fold outer edge over. Slip a wire loop inside the folds. Roll the ribbon around the base twice.

2. Fold ribbon back diagonally. Roll rose center over fold, keeping upper edge of rose center just below upper edge of fold. Roll to end of fold, forming a petal. Wrap tightly with floral wire.

3. Repeat step 2, until rose is desired size; cut ribbon from reel. Fold back ribbon end diagonally and secure to base. Wrap base with floral tape, continuing down stem.

For a traditional rose without a stem, omit the stem wire. Stitch the rose center to the backing fabric. Work the ribbon around the base, tacking it in place as you go.

HOW TO MAKE
FLOWER CENTERS

Artificial Stamens: Knot double thread around center of stamen cluster, or wrap floral wire around center, if making flowers with wired stems. Bend cluster in half; secure to flower center.

Ribbon Knots: Tie a small knot in the center of a short piece of narrow ribbon. Pull tails through flower center; secure to backing under flower or catch under floral tape of wired stem.

Beaded Stamens: String bugle beads on beading thread for stamen, add seed bead or oat bead at end, and run wire back down through stamen. Repeat for multiple stamens, stitching each to the flower center.

Pearls: Glue three or five pearls together in a cluster to the flower center. Or string small pearls on fine craft wire and form loops; twist wire ends together and secure to flower center.

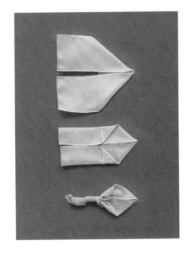

HOW TO MAKE A
FOLDED RIBBON LEAF

1. Cut a length of ribbon equal to three ribbon widths. Fold the ends down diagonally at the center; fold the outer edges in.

2. Pleat across the bottom, and twist tightly, if using wired ribbon. Or stitch running stitches across the bottom, catching the lower edge of the back; gather and knot.

HOW TO MAKE A PULLED
WIRE RIBBON LEAF

1. Cut a length of ribbon equal to six ribbon widths. Pull up on the wire from both ends of one side, gathering ribbon evenly toward the center.

2. Pleat across the bottom, and twist the wire tightly around the end. Glue or stitch the gathered edges together in the center of the leaf.

Silk Ribbon Embroidery

SILK ribbon embroidery, perhaps accented with beading, is a popular treatment for a padded headpiece. Narrow silk ribbons are sewn to fabric using a variety of unique stitches that create graceful, alluring curves and delicate dimensional designs. Silk ribbons are most commonly used in 2 mm, 4 mm, and 7 mm widths. Crewel needles, sizes 1 to 3, and chenille needles, sizes 18 to 24, are used; the needle eye must accommodate the full width of the ribbon. Patterns are marked on fabric using light pencil marks or a water-soluble marking pen. The fabric is held taut in an embroidery hoop, preventing the stitches from puckering the fabric, and the embroidery is completed before the fabric is cut to size and applied to the headpiece.

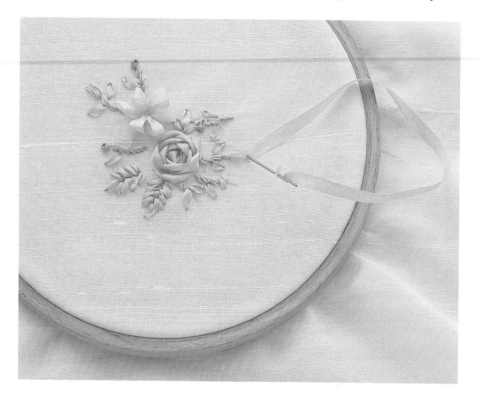

ABOVE *Using an assortment of the stitches shown opposite, a delicate floral pattern can be designed and embroidered to fit any headpiece.*

TIP *Keep your stitches loose, allowing the ribbon to form soft, sumptuous curves, curls, and loops on the fabric surface.*

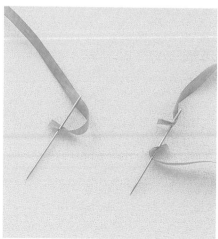

HOW TO BEGIN AND END

1. Thread an 18" (46 cm) length of ribbon through the eye of the needle. Pierce the center of the ribbon ¼" (6 mm) from the threaded end; pull the long end of the ribbon, locking the ribbon on the needle eye.

2. Fold over the free end of the ribbon ¼" (6 mm), and pierce the center of both layers with the needle. Draw the needle and ribbon through, forming a soft knot at the ribbon end.

3. Stitch until just before the ribbon gets too short. End the ribbon by running the needle to the underside of the fabric; draw the ribbon across the nearest stitch. Piercing both layers, take two small stitches to lock the ribbon. Trim off the ribbon tail.

STITCHES

Straight Stitch: Bring the needle up from the underside; pull the ribbon all the way through. Go down the desired distance away, keeping the ribbon flat. Make running stitches by continuing in a straight line, with small spaces between stitches. Make straight stitches that radiate from a single point to create a flower or bud.

Ribbon Stitch: Bring the needle up from the underside; pull the ribbon all the way through. Smooth the ribbon flat in the direction of the stitch. Insert the needle at the end of the stitch, piercing the center of the ribbon. Pull the needle through to the underside until the ribbon curls inward at the tip. Take care not to pull the ribbon too tight.

Lazy Daisy: Bring the needle up from the underside at the petal base; insert the needle right next to the exit point, and bring the needle back up at the petal tip. Pull the ribbon through the fabric, forming a small, smooth loop. Pass the ribbon over the loop; secure it with a small straight stitch at the tip.

Loop Stitch: Bring the needle up from the underside; pull ribbon through. Loop the ribbon smoothly over a holder, such as a trolley needle or large plastic darning needle held in the hand opposite the needle hand. Insert the needle into the fabric right in front of the exit point. Pull the ribbon through the fabric until the loop tightens around the holder. Continue to hold the completed loop until the next stitch is taken.

Stem Stitch: Bring the needle up through the fabric at the start of the marked or imaginary stem; make a small straight stitch. Bring the needle back through the fabric partway back and alongside the previous stitch. Repeat continuously for the desired length; keep the ribbon smooth without twisting.

Spider Web Rose: 1. Draw a circle with five evenly spaced spokes. Using embroidery floss or 2 mm ribbon, form a stitch along each of the spokes and tie off. 2. Bring the ribbon up at the center of the web. Weave the ribbon over and under the spokes in a circular fashion, working gradually outward, until the spokes are covered and the desired fullness achieved. Keep the ribbon loose; twists in the ribbon add interest. Push the needle through to the back and secure.

French Knot: Bring the needle up from the underside; pull ribbon through. Holding needle parallel to the fabric near the exit point, wrap ribbon once or twice around the needle; take care to keep ribbon smooth. Insert needle very close to the exit point, holding ribbon in place close to wrapped needle. Hold ribbon while pulling needle through to underside, releasing ribbon as it disappears and forms a soft knot.

Floral Supplies & Techniques

ABOVE *Rice flowers, eucalyptus seeds, and myrtle fill out the front and sides of this wreath; freesia and roses are clustered at the back.*

ABOVE *Rice flowers, eucalyptus seeds, and myrtle fill out the front and sides of this wreath; freesia and roses are clustered at the back.*

FRESH flowers, worn in the hair, once symbolized earth's abundance and promised fertility. Today, many brides simply prefer the feminine, romantic style that fresh flowers impart. A floral wreath, a cluster of flowers wired to a barrette, or individual flowers secured to hair picks can work well with a formal or informal wedding and complement any dress. Flowers can add lovely, soft colors around the bride's face to play up the blush in her cheeks. Or they can follow a strictly white palette, in keeping with the rest of her attire. The bride also has the option of wearing them with or without a veil, which can be attached to a comb.

Fresh flower hair accessories, minus any ribbon elements, can be prepared one or two days before the wedding, misted with water, and kept in a plastic bag in the refrigerator. Ribbon bows or streamers can be added just before the wedding. For best results, order flowers from a florist; these will come specially treated to last. Select a primary flower type, an optional secondary flower, an optional novelty material, one or two greens of different textures, and a filler material. The number of flowers needed depends on the size and desired fullness of the headpiece and the size of the flowers. Cut off 1/2" to 1" (1.3 to 2.5 cm) of the stems at an angle, using a sharp knife, not a scissors. Put the stems into a vase of fresh, tepid water mixed with flower preservative. Rose stems must be placed into water immediately after cutting, to prevent air bubbles from forming in the stems.

FRESH FLOWER SUGGESTIONS	
Flower	Sweetheart (miniature) or hybrid (standard) roses, miniature carnations, ranunculus, freesia, and chrysanthemums (daisy and other varieties)
Greens	Italian ruscus, plumosa fern, variegated ittosporum, cedar, smilax, euonymus, eucalyptus, leatherleaf fern, ivy, camellia, myrtle
Novelties	Hypernium berries, rose hips, eucalyptus seeds
Fillers	Baby's breath, limonium or caspia, statice, Queen Anne's lace, rice flowers

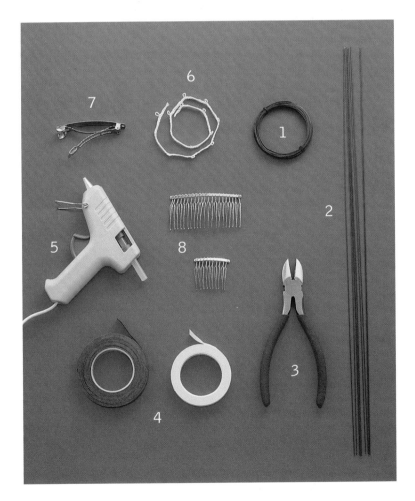

Along with fresh flowers, greens, and ribbons, there are a few other supplies necessary for making floral hair accessories. Wreath frames are formed from 20-gauge FLORIST WIRE (1); individual flowers and greens are wired to 24-gauge STEM WIRE (2) for support. A WIRE CUTTER (3) should be used to cut the wires. FLORAL TAPE (4), available in white or green, is used to wrap the flowers to the stem wires and ultimately to the wreath or barrette. Green tape is suitable for most accessories; white tape may be used for an all-white theme without greens. A HOT GLUE GUN (5) is used to attach BUTTONHOLE LOOPS (6) to a wreath for securing to the hair with bobby pins. CLIP-STYLE BARRETTES (7) and WIRE COMBS (8) work well for small floral hair accessories.

4. Place the end of floral tape on the back side of the flower calyx, as close to the flower head as possible; hold it in place with the index finger. Wrap the tape once around the stem, gently stretching the tape; press the tape onto itself. The warmth of the fingers softens the paraffin in the tape, causing it to stick.

5. Twist the flower, so the tape spirals around the stem; pull the tape gently, stretching and warming it between the thumb and index finger. Work the tape down the stem to the bottom of the wire, wrapping at a slight downward angle. Break off the tape and smooth it over the wire end.

HOW TO WIRE FLOWERS WITH A DEEP CALYX

1. Cut off the flower stem about 1" (2.5 cm) below the flower head.

2. Cut a 24-gauge stem wire in half. Pierce the flower through the side of the calyx, just below the flower head, with the wire. Push the wire through the calyx to the wire center, and bend both ends down along the stem.

3. For large flowers, such as standard roses, insert the remaining wire through the calyx at a right angle to the first wire, if the flower bends over or is wobbly when it is held upright.

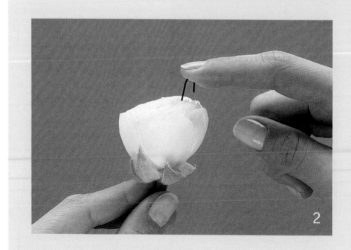

HOW TO WIRE A FLOWER WITH A SHALLOW CALYX

1. Follow step 1, above. Cut a 24-gauge floral stem wire in half. Bend one end into a small hook.

2. Pierce the center top of the flower with the straight end of the wire. Gently push the wire down through the flower and stem until the hook disappears inside the flower. Tape the flower as in steps 4 and 5, above.

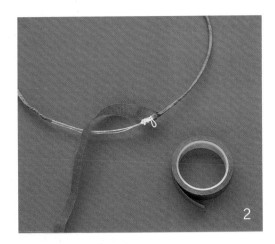

HOW TO SECURE FLOWERS TO A BARRETTE OR COMB

1. Prepare an odd number of flower clusters, depending on the barrette or comb size, as in step 3 at left. Remove the tension bar from a barrette, and wrap floral tape twice around one end, stretching and warming it to secure. Or secure the tape to one end of a comb.

2. Tape the stems of the first flower cluster to the barrette or comb, allowing the flower head to extend off the end; wrap the tape between the teeth of a comb. Tape the next cluster to the barrette or comb, in the same direction, overlapping the first cluster slightly. Repeat, ending just below the flower head of the center cluster. Tear off the floral tape and secure the end onto itself.

3. Repeat step 2, beginning from the opposite end. As stems coming from opposite directions overlap, wrap floral tape around both. Continue to stopping point in step 2; tear off tape and secure to itself.

4. Wrap the ends of any free-hanging stems to the barrette or comb; carefully maneuver the tape between the flowers. Bend the clusters into the desired positions.

HOW TO MAKE A FRESH FLOWER HAIR WREATH

1. Wrap 20-gauge wire three times around in a circle of the desired size, twisting it together slightly, for the wreath base. Try it on for size, allowing ½" (1.3 cm) of ease that will be taken up by the floral tape wrapping, slightly more if a veil will be attached. Wrap the wire circle with floral tape.

2. Glue four or more button loops, evenly spaced, to the inside of the base, for bobby pins. Wrap the loop ends to the base, using floral tape.

3. Wire and tape 20 to 30 flowers as shown opposite. Encircle each wired flower back with pieces of filler flower, 1½" to 2" (3.8 to 5 cm) long; join them to the taped flower stem, using one or two wraps of floral tape. Repeat with the greens, forming a tight, elliptical cluster.

4. Tape the first cluster to the base 1" (2.5 cm) from the center back; hold the flower below the head, and tape the stem flat onto the base. Tape the next cluster to the base, in the same direction, overlapping the first cluster slightly and hiding the base. Continue around the base; avoid covering the button loops. Tuck the stems of the last clusters under the heads of the first cluster.

BRIDAL pearls come in a variety of shapes and sizes. The most common are round pearls, sized from 2 mm to 10 mm, and oval pearls, called oats, ranging from 3 mm to 10 mm. Pear-shaped pearl drops, in various sizes, are popular for dangling accents on headpieces. BRIDAL PEARLS (1) are actually glass or plastic beads that have been dipped in paint to give the appearance of a natural pearl. The quality of the paint job determines the quality and price of the pearl. Inexpensive bridal pearls, suitable for gluing to headpieces or veils, or when used in large quantities, can be purchased at fabric and craft stores. However, if you are investing a great deal of time in the headpiece and want it to become an heirloom, you may want to shop at a specialty bead store and inquire about the quality of the beads you intend to purchase.

CRYSTALS (2) also vary in quality; they range from plastic to glass to true Austrian crystals, which can cost several dollars apiece. Their faceted surfaces reflect light and add a lot of sparkle to a headpiece. Some crystals are clear; others may have an iridescent finish that reflects a rainbow of sheer colors. They are found in many shapes, including round, bugles, and drops, and in a wide range of sizes. For similar effect, RHINESTONES (3) secured together on a flexible metal strip are often attached to headpieces. Other beads suitable for bridal headpieces include METALLICS and GLASS SEED BEADS (4).

Pearls and crystals can be purchased in various sizes and forms. They may be packaged loose or strung loosely on cotton string to be separated and used one at a time. For applications that require a continuous row of beads, they may be glued or fused to a string or braided onto cross-locked strands that can be cut without the beads falling off. They can be glued to headpieces, sewn to veil edges, or woven on fine wire to form one-of-a-kind headpieces.

A METAL HEADBAND FORM (5) provides a base for wiring beads and rhinestones to make a bejeweled headpiece. When finished, it can be worn as a headband or the teeth can be bent inward and it can be worn as a tiara. A METAL BALL NECKLACE or CHOKER (6), available in silver or gold at craft stores or jewelry stores, can be used in a similar way to make a crown or bun wrap. For these techniques, you will also need JEWELRY WIRE (7) in various gauges, from 24 to 28; the higher the number, the thinner the wire. Use thicker wire for larger beads or when the wire only has to pass through the bead once. Use thinner wire when working with seed beads or when the wire passes through some of the beads two or three times. Jewelry wire should be cut with a WIRE CUTTER or HEAVY-DUTY CRAFT SCISSORS (8); NEEDLENOSE PLIERS (9) may be necessary for creating tight loops.

5

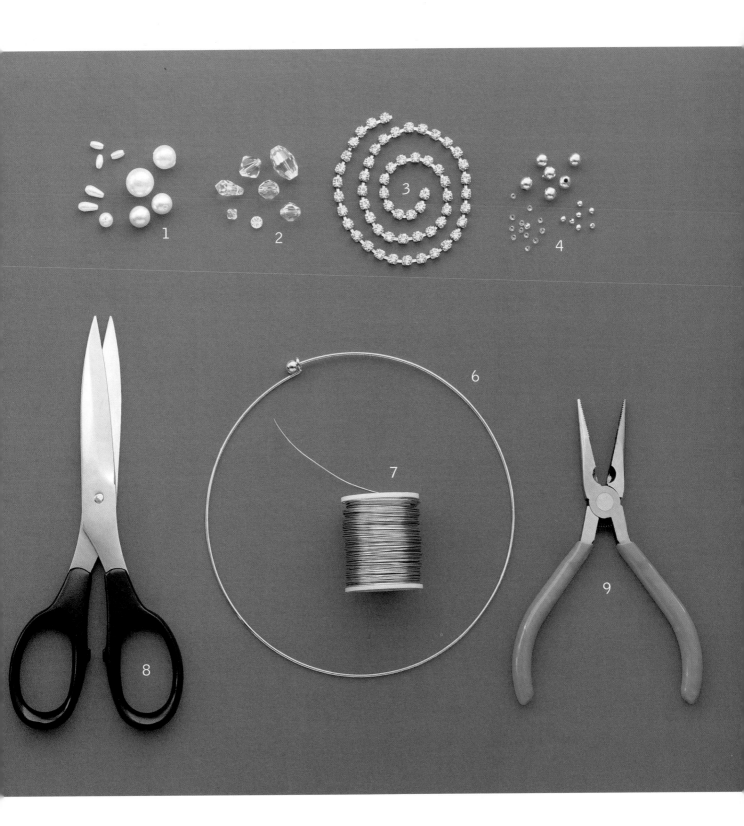

Beadwork

HOW TO MAKE A BEADED HEADBAND

Method #1:

1. Cut an 18" (46 cm) piece of wire; secure one end to the base in a cross-lock pattern.

2. Thread four beads onto the wire; insert the wire back through the first bead, forming a tight loop. Pull the wire, snugging the loop against the front of the base; wrap the wire once around the base, between the teeth.

3. Repeat step 2, packing the bead loops as closely as desired. For more texture, use a larger bead as the third bead. Or string more beads on some of the loops. Start new wire lengths as needed, cross-locking as in step 1. Finish by cross-locking; thread the wire tail under the wrapped wire and cut off. Arrange the bead loops as desired.

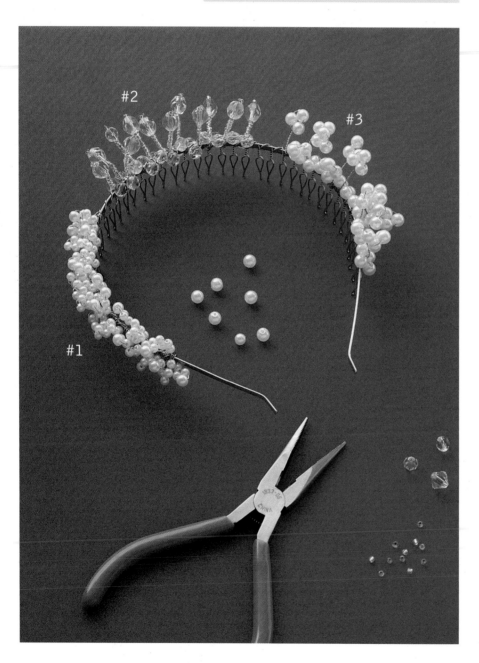

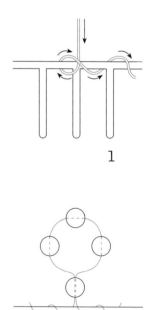

Method #2:

1. Cut an 18" (46 cm) piece of 28-gauge wire; secure one end to the base in a cross-lock pattern.

2. Thread 6 to 10 seed beads or other small beads onto the wire. Add a large bead and one more small one. Thread the wire back through the large bead and the row of small beads; pull tight, so bead dangle is snug to the base. Wrap the wire around the base.

3. Thread one large bead (diameter equal to or larger than the base width) onto the wire. Holding the bead against the front of the base, wrap the wire once around the base. Alternatively, secure two or three beads at a time that, together, would cover the base.

4. Repeat steps 2 and 3, packing the beads closely. Vary the length of the dangles or add seed bead loops (method #1) to add interest. Start new wire lengths as needed, cross-locking as in step 1. Finish by cross-locking; thread the wire tail under the wrapped wire and cut off. Arrange the bead dangles as desired.

Method #3:

1. Cut an 18" (46 cm) piece of wire; secure one end to the base in a cross-lock pattern.

2. Thread three beads onto the wire. Bring the wire back down to the base, forming a loop, with the beads held ½" to 1" (1.3 to 2.5 cm) from the base.

3. Turn the beads, twisting the wires together, until the twist is snug against the beads and base. Wrap the loose end around the base.

4. Thread one large bead (diameter equal to or larger than the base width) onto the wire. Holding the bead against the front of the base, wrap the wire once around the base. Alternatively, secure two or three beads at a time that, together, would cover the base.

5. Repeat steps 2 to 4, packing the beads closely. Vary the length of the twisted clusters to add interest. Start new wire lengths as needed, cross-locking as in step 1. Finish by cross-locking; thread the wire tail under the wrapped wire and cut off. Arrange the bead clusters as desired.

HOW TO ATTACH CONTINUOUS RHINESTONES

1. Secure the wire end to the base in a cross-lock pattern. Feed the wire from the spool rather than cutting a piece. Hold the rhinestones against the base; wrap wire around the base and rhinestones, wrapping once in each space. Finish by cross-locking; thread the wire tail under the wrapped wire and cut off.

2. Alternately, work bead loops (method #1), bead dangles (method #2), or bead clusters (method #3) in the spaces between rhinestones.

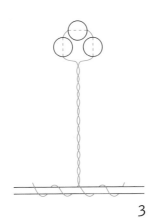

2

3

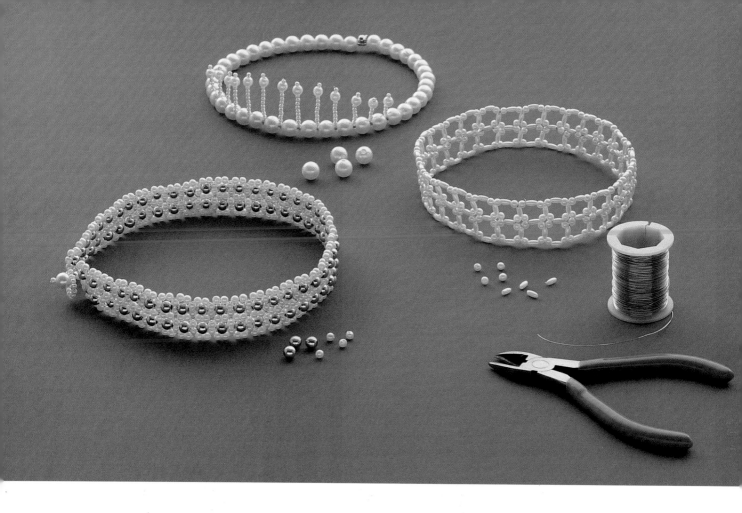

HOW TO MAKE A BEADED CROWN OR BUN WRAP

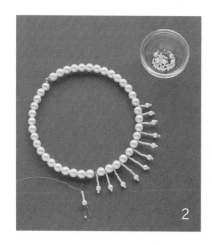

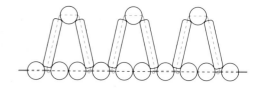

1. Unscrew the ball from the closure of a wire ball necklace. Slide beads onto the wire; the beads must have a hole large enough to slide onto the wire easily. Reattach the ball.

2. Add loops, clusters, or dangles between beads, as on pages 46 and 47, beginning at the end opposite the ball. Run the wire through the large beads rather than crossing over them. Remove a bead from the ball end to create more space, if necessary.

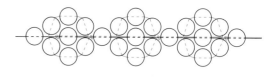

   Alternately, work other bead patterns as shown in the diagrams at right, wrapping the wire between the base beads or inserting it through them as necessary. To keep arcs and peaks from falling, wrap the wire around the base in opposite directions at the beginning and end of each one.

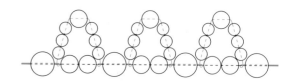

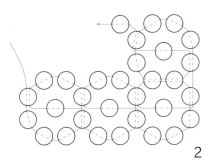

2

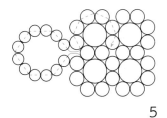

HOW TO MAKE A DAISY CHAIN BUN WRAP

1. Cut 28-gauge wire 28" (71 cm) long. Form a small loop 10" (25.5 cm) from one end to keep the beads from falling off. From the opposite end, thread eight 4 mm round beads; form into a circle by going back through the first one.

2. Add a 6 mm bead; insert the wire through the fifth bead. Continue, following the diagram to the desired length of the bun wrap. Join new wire lengths by twisting the new wire to the old one, and thread the tails back through the design.

3. If a second row is desired, turn the design and work backward, following the diagram.

4. To make a bead closure, thread one small bead onto the center of an 8" (20.5 cm) length of wire; Fold the wire in half and thread both ends onto a large bead and two small beads. Thread the wires through the center of one end of the bun wrap; wrap several time to secure, and cut.

5. Thread 12 small beads onto the 10" (25.5 cm) loose wire at the opposite end; make a loop, and secure to the bun wrap.

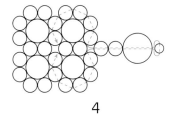

4

5

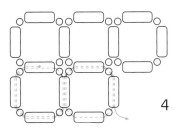

3

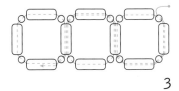

4

HOW TO MAKE A WOVEN PEARL BUN WRAP

1. Cut an 18" (46 cm) piece of 28-gauge wire; form a small loop in one end to keep beads from falling off.

2. String a 4 mm round bead and a 6 mm oat bead; repeat three times. Feed the wire back through the first six beads, forming a square.

3. Follow the diagram to weave the beads. Join new wire lengths by twisting the new wire to the old one, and thread the tails back through the design. Continue to the desired length. Join the beginning to the end.

4. Work another row of squares alongside the first row, following the diagram. Work wire ends into the design to finish.

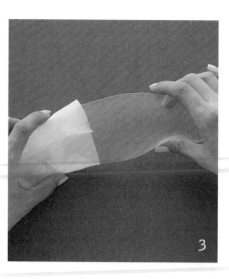

Bows

MANY a bride prefers the simplicity of wearing a single bow in her hair. Versatile and adaptable, bows can be made in many different styles, fashioned from fabric, lace, or ribbon. A bow can be an embellishment for a headpiece or it can be attached to a barrette or comb to be worn alone, with or without a veil or pouf. A plain bow may even provide the foundation for an arrangement of silk or fresh flowers or other trimmings. Bows made from wire-edge ribbon will keep their shape nicely. Limp fabrics, like crepe or charmeuse, can be given extra body with horsehair braid; the bow width must be the same as the horsehair, which comes in various sizes. Crisp fabrics, like satin or taffeta, have enough body alone. For a unique look, the bow edges can be finished with pearls or cross-locked glass beads (page 78) or with lace edging (page 80). A silk ribbon embroidery (page 38) design can be worked on the front of a fabric bow.

HOW TO MAKE A SINGLE FABRIC BOW

1. Cut a rectangle of fabric two times longer than the desired bow length and twice the desired width plus ½" (1.3 cm). For a softer look or for a bow that will be stiffened with horsehair, cut the strip on the bias.

2. Fold the fabric in half, lengthwise, right sides together. Stitch the long edges together in a ¼" (6 mm) seam. Press the seam allowances open using the tip of the iron down the center of the seam; avoid pressing the outer folds. Turn the tube right side out.

3. Center the seam on one side of the tube. To stiffen the bow, cut horsehair braid the length of the tube; wrap cut end with masking tape. Slide horsehair into the tube. With the seam facing up, fold the tube ends to the center.

4. Using a double thread, hand-baste through all layers, up one side of center and down the other. Pull up on the thread to gather the bow center; knot the ends together.

5. Cut a fabric rectangle twice the desired width of the knot and 1" (2.5 cm) longer than the circumference of the center. Fold the long edges to the center; press lightly. Wrap the fabric around the bow center; turn one end under and overlap the other at the bow back. Hand-stitch in place.

6. Hand-stitch or glue the ribbon back to a barrette or comb. For added stability on large bows, hand-stitch a comb to the back of each loop, angling the combs slightly outward.

RIGHT *With a little creativity, bows in endless variety can be made from fabric, ribbon, or lace.*

HOW TO MAKE A
DOUBLE FABRIC BOW

1. Follow steps 1 and 2 on page
50 for a single fabric bow. Cut a
second rectangle 1" (2.5 cm) shorter
than the first; follow steps 1 and 2
for the second.

2. Follow step 3 for both tubes;
layer the short one over the longer
one; aligning centers. Follow step 4,
stitching through all layers. Finish
the bow as in steps 5 and 6.

HOW TO MAKE A SINGLE
RIBBON OR LACE BOW

1. Cut a length of ribbon or lace twice
the desired length of the bow plus
1" (2.5 cm). With the wrong side facing
up, fold the ends to the center; overlap
the ends 1/2" (1.3 cm).

2. Using a double thread, hand-baste
through all the layers, up one side of
center and down the other. Pull up on
the thread to gather the bow center;
knot the ends together.

3. Cut a length of ribbon or lace
for the knot, 1" (2.5 cm) longer than
the center circumference. Wrap the
knot around the bow center; turn one
end under and overlap the other at
the back. Hand-stitch in place.

4. If tails are desired for a ribbon
bow, slip a length of ribbon between
the knot and bow back, gathering
it at the center; tack or glue in place.
Angle-cut the ribbon ends at slightly
different lengths, with the shorter
edges outward. If necessary, apply a
thin line of liquid fray preventer to
the cut edges.

HOW TO MAKE A
MULTI-LAYER RIBBON BOW

1. Plan the bow so that each layer is
1/2" (1.3 cm) shorter than the one
beneath it. Cut one length of ribbon
equal to twice the length of all
the layers plus 1" (2.5 cm). Overlap
the ends 1/2" (1.3 cm); pin to the
center of the ribbon.

2. Beginning with the bottom layer,
crease the ribbon, right sides
together, a distance from the center
equal to the length of the bottom
layer; repeat for the other side. Bring
the creases to the center, forming
loops, and pin.

3. Repeat step 2 for each set of
loops. Finish the bow, following steps
2 to 4, at left, basting through all
the ribbon layers in step 2.

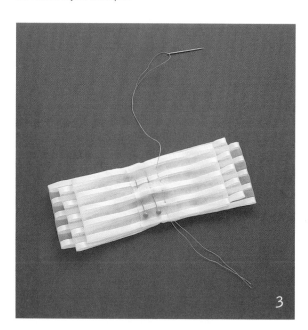

3

TIP *To ensure that your
barrette will not slip out of
place, secure a narrow strip of
self-adhesive foam to the
surface of the tension bar.*

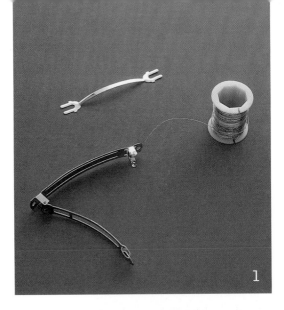

1

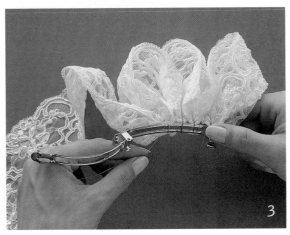

3

HOW TO MAKE A MULTI-LOOP LACE BOW

1. Remove the tension bar from a barrette. Leaving wire on the spool, insert beading wire into the hole at the barrette end; twist to secure.

2. Cut a 1 yd. (0.92 m) length of galloon lace, 3" to 5" (7.5 to 12.7 cm) wide. Pinch together one end; wrap three times with wire to the end of the barrette, with the raw edges pointing inward.

3. Make loop; pinch together the loop base, and secure to barrette, wrapping wire three times. Repeat, making four more loops. Turn the raw edges inward when securing the last loop. Secure wire to the hole at the other end of the barrette; trim off excess. Replace tension bar.

HOW TO MAKE A MULTI-LOOP RIBBON BOW

1. Attach wire to the barrette as in step 1, left. Cut a 1½ yd. (1.4 m) length of ribbon, ⅝" to 1½" (15 to 39 mm) wide. Wire one end of the ribbon to the barrette, leaving a 2½" (6.5 cm) tail extending outward.

2. Secure about 11 ribbon loops as in step 3, left, pointing the first loop up, the second loop down, and the third loop to the center; repeat the pattern to the end of the barrette. Secure the end to the barrette, leaving a 2½" (6.5 cm) tail extending outward.

3. Adjust the loops evenly along the barrette; trim the tails as desired, and apply liquid fray preventer to the raw edges. Replace tension bar.

Optional Streamers:
Cut three 12" (30.5 cm) and two 10" (25.5 cm) streamers from ⅛" (3 mm) ribbon. Tie love knots in the ends of the streamers and at staggered distances from the ends. Layer the ribbons, and hot-glue to the center underside of the barrette.

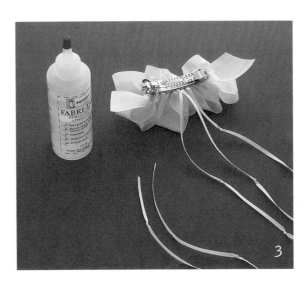

3

Designing a Veil

ABUNDANT options for veil styles, lengths, and embellishments make it possible to design a one-of-a-kind veil that complements your wedding gown and headpiece to perfection. Consider what silhouette you want the veil to create, in combination with the dress. A high pouffed veil, for instance, can balance a full-skirted gown, while dresses with straighter silhouettes call for veils that hug the body more closely. A veil can be used to add height, which can be a positive thing unless it causes the bride to overshadow the groom. To minimize height, a mantilla-style veil can be worn. The fullness of the veil depends, in part, on the width of illusion used and also on the number of layers. For a simple, slender look, the veil can be a single layer of narrow illusion, attached at the back of the head. Multi-tier, bouffant, circular, and cascade veils create a fuller silhouette, especially when they radiate from higher on the bride's head.

The headpiece style, its position on the head, and the location of the veil attachment all influence how the veil will fall. If the veil is attached to the back of a crown, bun wrap, or wreath, for example, it will fan out across the back. A veil that is attached at the top of the head to a headband, crescent, or Juliet cap can fall over the front of the shoulders; this may require more fullness, especially for fingertip or longer veils. If you want to wear a blusher veil as you approach the altar, a cascade or full-circle veil attached at the top of the head is necessary. For added height, select a bouffant veil that attaches behind the front of a crown or to a headband or decorative comb worn on top of the head.

Veil Lengths

Shoulder or Flyaway

Elbow

Fingertip

Ballet or Waltz

Chapel

Cathedral

VEILS fall into several standard categories for length; which length you select is influenced by the style of the gown and the formality of the wedding. Full-skirted gowns are better balanced with longer veils; sleek dress silhouettes look better with shorter veils. If the veil is shorter than chapel length, plan for it to end below the design features on the back of the dress, such as a low V-back, peplum, or a row of satin roses; the dress details will be visible through the sheer illusion. In general, longer veils are worn for more formal weddings, in grand or solemn settings that instill a feeling of pageantry. Shorter veils are more casual and unconventional; they are also suitable for second-time brides.

Bridal veil lengths are measured from the point of attachment on the headpiece to a specific point on the bride's body. While ready-made veils are produced in industry standard lengths that are often too long for most brides, making the veil allows you to cut it at the exact length suitable for the bride.

Two-tier and three-tier veils can be made so all tiers fall to the same length. Or each tier can fall to one of the standard lengths; the longest tier being the under-most layer and the shortest tier being the top layer.

BRIDAL VEIL LENGTHS

Shoulder or Flyaway	Touches the shoulders; usual length for a blusher
Elbow	Touches elbows when arms are straight at the sides
Fingertip	Touches fingertips when arms are straight at the sides
Ballet or Waltz	Falls to mid-calf or just above the ankles
Chapel	Brushes the floor
Cathedral	Trails on the floor; 3 yd. to 5 yd. (2.75 to 4.6 m) from the headpiece

Cutting & Pressing Nylon Illusion

NYLON illusion comes in widths of 72", 108", and 144" (183, 274.5, and 366 cm). The widest width is necessary for a full, chapel length or cathedral length veil, so the lower edge of the veil traces a wide arc on the floor. The narrower widths are suitable for most other veil styles, depending on how much fullness is desired. Illusion is folded several times before being rolled on cardboard bolts. Avoid buying from a bolt that is almost empty, especially if there are deep wrinkles in the illusion; it may be impossible to get them out. Instead, ask the salesperson to cut from a new bolt. Purchase a little extra for testing edge finishes. For ease in handling, recut the illusion at home to the exact length needed without opening out the folds. Then refold the illusion to cut round corners, as directed in the steps specific for each veil style. Use a rotary cutter and cutting mat, if you have them.

Slight wrinkles in the illusion need not be pressed out before construction; you will undoubtedly acquire a few more as you work with it. Nylon melts easily, so be very careful when pressing. Test the iron temperature on scraps before touching the iron to the veil. As an alternative to pressing, steam the veil lightly with a hand-held steamer or hang it in a steamy bathroom and allow the wrinkles to fall out.

Veil Styles

THERE are several basic veil styles that vary in shape by the way the illusion is cut, by the number of layers used, and by the method of gathering at the point of attachment to the headpiece. The width of illusion used and the length of the veil also impact the veil's appearance. Patterns are not necessary, because full widths of illusion are used for each of the styles. The diagrams that accompany each style show how to fold the layers, how to round the corners, and where to gather. The measurements for veil length include a construction allowance. This accounts for length that will be "eaten up" by gathering the veil, attaching it to a headpiece, and applying an edge finish.

SINGLE-TIER VEIL *A single tier gives the veil a very sheer, understated look; use either 72" or 108" (183 or 274.5 cm) illusion, depending on the desired fullness. Or use 144" (366 cm) illusion for a full cathedral length veil. A single-tier veil can be attached to any headpiece or comb; the wider the attachment area, the more the veil will spread over the shoulders and back.*

HOW TO MAKE A SINGLE-TIER VEIL

1. Measure from point of attachment on the headpiece to desired length; add 2" (5 cm) for construction allowance. Cut the illusion.

2. Open out the illusion, and refold down the center, aligning the outer edges. Pin the layers together as necessary to keep the illusion from shifting.

3. On a large piece of paper, draw a quarter circle pattern with a radius or 36" (91.5 cm) for chapel or cathedral length veils, 24" (61 cm) for ballet or fingertip, or 18" (46 cm) for elbow or shoulder length. Place the pattern over the lower corner of the illusion, aligning the outer edges. Cut the illusion in a curve, following the pattern.

4. Apply an edge finish (pages 72 to 93) to the veil, if desired.

5. Thread a needle with double thread; knot the ends together. Fold over one corner of the upper edge diagonally, about ¼" (6 mm). Take a stitch through the fold; secure the thread by running the needle between the threads before pulling the knot tight.

6. Stitch across the upper edge of the veil, taking ¼" (6 mm) stitches that wrap around the veil edge, going about ¼" (6 mm) deep into the edge. Work the needle in a spiral pattern, inserting from the back to the front; fill the needle with stitches before pulling the thread through. Repeat across.

7. Pull up on the thread, gathering the veil edge to the desired width; knot the thread. Attach the veil to the headpiece or comb (page 70).

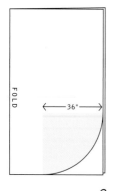

FOLD

← 36" →

3

5

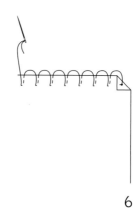

6

TWO-TIER VEIL *Two-tier veils are made from one long length of illusion, folded crosswise; illusion has no right or wrong side. The tiers can be made to the same length or to two different lengths, such as an elbow length underlayer and a shoulder length upper layer.*

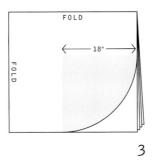

3

TIP For a veil with two layers of the same length, make the fold 1/2" (1.3 cm) off-center, with the shorter layer on top. This will help the layers separate better visually.

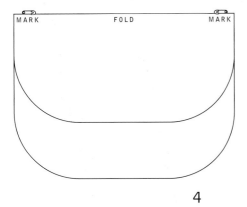

4

HOW TO MAKE A TWO-TIER VEIL

1. Measure from the point of attachment on the headpiece to the desired length of each layer plus 2" (5 cm) for construction allowance. Add the measurements together, and cut the illusion to the total length.

2. Open out the illusion, and refold down the center, aligning the outer edges; fold again in the opposite direction, aligning the four corners. Pin the layers together as necessary to keep the illusion from shifting.

3. On a large piece of paper, draw a quarter circle pattern, following the guidelines in step 3, opposite. Place the pattern over the lower corner of the illusion, aligning the outer edges. Cut the illusion in a curve, following the pattern.

4. Open out the veil. Fold crosswise into two layers of desired lengths; mark the sides of the veil with small safety pins at the fold. Apply an edge finish (pages 72 to 93) to the veil, if desired, beginning and ending the finish for each layer at the marks; make sure the finish is applied to the surface that will be facing outward.

5. Refold the veil at the marks; pin along the fold as necessary to keep the layers from shifting. Gather the upper edge as in steps 5 to 7, opposite, wrapping the stitches over the fold.

TWO-TIER VEIL WITH A POUF *Similar to a two-tier veil, this style has a pouf at the point of attachment to the headpiece, adding height and drawing more attention to the head. The veil is made from one long piece of illusion, folded crosswise; the gathering line, running a distance below the fold, creates the pouf. The tiers for this style can also be the same length or different lengths.*

HOW TO MAKE A TWO-TIER VEIL WITH A POUF

1. Determine the desired height of the pouf by folding a length of net crosswise; gather it in your hand 4" to 8" (10 to 20.5 cm) from the folded edge. Position the gathered net at the back of the headpiece; adjust the pouf height, and record the total length of net needed. Measure from the point of attachment on the headpiece to the desired length of each layer plus 2" (5 cm) for construction allowance. Add all the measurements together, and cut the illusion to the total length.

2. Follow steps 2 and 3 on page 59 for rounding the veil corners.

3. Open out the veil. Fold crosswise into two layers of desired lengths, adding half the pouf allowance to each length; mark the sides of both layers of the veil with small safety pins at the bottom of the pouf. Apply an edge finish (pages 72 to 93) to the veil, if desired, beginning and ending the finish for each layer at the marks; make sure the finish is applied to the surface that will be facing outward.

4. Refold the veil, aligning the marks; pin along the fold as necessary to keep the layers from shifting. Thread a needle with double thread; knot the ends together. Take a stitch through both layers at the marks on one side of the veil; secure the thread by running the needle between the threads before pulling the knot tight.

5. Hand-stitch a gathering row through both layers, with the distance from the folded edge equal to the height of the pouf. Pull up on the thread, gathering the veil edge to the desired width; knot the thread. Attach the veil to the headpiece or comb (page 70). Separate the layers of illusion in the pouf.

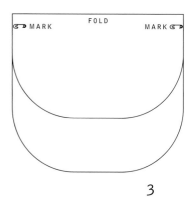

3

TIP *The veil edge finish can continue onto the right side of the pouf edges, but be aware that it creates two definite loops that can look like ears!*

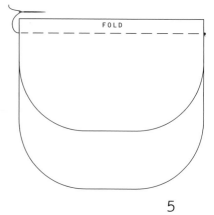

5

HOW TO MAKE A
BOUFFANT VEIL

1. Measure from the point of attachment on the headpiece plus 2" (5 cm) for construction allowance; add 12" (30.5 cm) for the bouffant effect, and cut the illusion to the total length.

2. Round the lower corners as in steps 2 and 3 for a single-tier veil, page 58. With the veil still folded in half lengthwise, place a safety pin 12" (30.5 cm) from the top on the cut edges. Mark a gentle arch from the pin to the top, ending at the fold. Cut along the curved line.

3. Apply an edge finish (pages 72 to 93) to the veil, if desired. Finish the veil as in steps 5 to 7 on page 58.

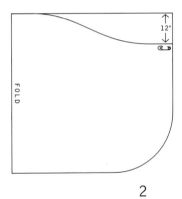

2

BOUFFANT VEIL *The upper edge of a bouffant veil is cut in an arch that allows the illusion to billow up over the head. This is suitable for veils attached to the top or close to the front of the head, perhaps behind the front of a crown or tiara. If a two-tier bouffant veil is desired, cut the tiers to different lengths, and gather them together as one. If only the top layer is bouffant, prepare the tiers separately and attach them together to the headpiece.*

THREE-TIER VEIL *Combine the methods for the single-tier and two-tier veils; fold one long piece of illusion to create the top two tiers and add a single layer beneath them. Gather all three layers together as one.*

CASCADE VEIL *The cascade veil is a two-tier veil that falls in gentle folds to two different lengths. It is gathered only in the center of the fold, not from edge to edge. As a result, the leading edge of the veil, falling from the headpiece next to the face, is a gentle fold of illusion, not a cut edge. The upper layer can be folded forward over the face and worn as a blusher; the veil edge traces a soft line just above the bustline, over the arms, and down to the desired length in the back.*

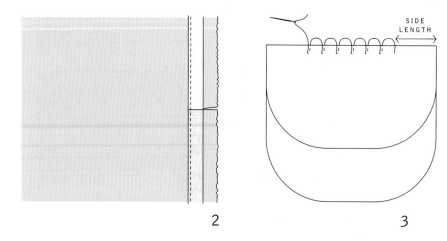

SIDE
LENGTH

2   3

HOW TO MAKE A CASCADE VEIL

1. Follow steps 1 to 3 for a two-tier veil, page 59. If the upper layer will be worn as a blusher, measure from the point of attachment, over the face, to the desired length. Open out the veil. Fold crosswise into two layers of desired lengths; mark the sides of the veil with small safety pins at the fold.

2. Apply a continuous edge finish (pages 72 to 93) to the veil, if desired, camouflaging the joint. For best results, avoid finishes that are not reversible. If applying a narrow ribbon edge, stop with the needle down in the ribbon at the mark; raise the presser foot. Clip the net up to the needle, slip the ribbon under the net, and continue stitching, with the net on top. At the opposite mark, reverse the procedure and stitch with the ribbon on top, so that the ribbon will be on the outside when the blusher is flipped back.

3. Refold the veil at the marks; pin along the fold as necessary to keep the layers from shifting. On the fold, mark a distance from the outer edge equal to the desired veil side length; repeat on the opposite side. Knot thread at one mark. Gather the folded edge between the marks as in steps 6 and 7 on page 58, wrapping the stitches over the fold.

MANTILLA *A mantilla is a complete circle of netting, attached at the front of the head with a wide comb. Originally, Spanish mantillas were made entirely of lace and were worn over a high decorative headpiece. This look can be achieved by cutting the veil from a wide piece of Chantilly or other fine lace fabric and finishing the entire circle with a galloon or edging lace. Customarily, the mantilla is worn with the leading edge at the hairline or falling over the forehead. The circle can be cut in any size, from 36" to 108" (91.5 to 274.5 cm).*

1. Measure the desired mantilla size from the leading edge on the front hairline or forehead to the longest point in the back. Subtract twice the lace edging width. Cut the illusion or lace fabric to this length.

2. Open out the illusion or lace, and refold down the center, aligning the outer edges; fold again in the opposite direction, aligning four corners. Pin the layers together as necessary to keep the illusion or lace from shifting.

3. Tie a long string to a pushpin and insert the pin into the work surface at the upper point of the folds. Tie the other end to a fabric marker a distance from the pin equal to the desired mantilla radius (half the total length determined in step 1). Draw an arc on the illusion or lace, keeping the marker upright and the string taut between the pushpin and the marker. Cut on the marked line.

4. Apply a wide lace edge finish (page 81), shaping the lace around the curve. Hand-stitch the leading edge of the mantilla to a large comb, hiding the stitches in the lace. Or attach it over the outer surface of a crescent or Juliet cap.

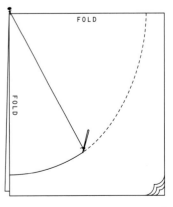

3

TIP *Only 1" (2.5 cm) of construction allowance is needed for circular veils because there is less fullness at the point of attachment.*

HALF-CIRCLE VEIL *A half-circle veil has less fullness at the point of attachment and flares out along the lower edge. Contemporary in style, it is a good choice when the gown back has interesting detailing or for showcasing embroidery or passementerie along the veil edges. Cut from 108" (274.5 cm) wide illusion, the veil will fall to the fingertips; cut from 72" (183 cm) illusion, it will brush the shoulders. This style also works for a chapel or cathedral length sheer veil, if cut from 144" (366 cm) illusion.*

ELONGATED HALF-CIRCLE VEIL
The half circle can be elongated so the veil falls to one point on the sides and to a longer point at the back. Select the illusion width to correspond to the desired length at the side.

HOW TO MAKE A HALF-CIRCLE VEIL

1. Measure from the point of attachment on the headpiece to the desired length plus 1" (2.5 cm) for construction allowance; add 14" (35.5 cm), and cut the illusion to the total length.

2. Open out the illusion, and refold down the center, aligning the outer edges. Pin the layers together as necessary to keep the illusion from shifting.

3. Tie a long string to a pushpin and insert it into the work surface at the upper end of the fold. Tie the other end to a fabric marker a distance from the pin equal to the desired finished veil length plus 15" (38 cm). Draw an arc on the illusion, keeping the marker upright and the string taut between the pushpin and the marker. Cut on the marked line.

4. Retie the string to the marker 14" (35.5 cm) from the pushpin. Draw a smaller arc, and cut the illusion.

5. Apply an edge finish (pages 72 to 93) to the veil, if desired; begin and end at the edges of the small cut curve, pivoting at the front corners. Finish the veil as in steps 5 to 7 on page 58, gathering along the small cut curve.

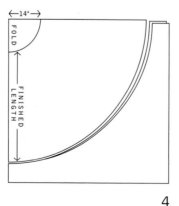

4

HOW TO MAKE AN ELONGATED HALF-CIRCLE VEIL

1. Measure from the point of attachment on the headpiece to the longest point desired at the veil back plus 1" (2.5 cm) for construction allowance; add 14" (35.5 cm), and cut the illusion to the total length.

2. Open out the illusion, and refold down the center, aligning outer edges. Pin the layers together to keep the illusion from shifting. Cut away the upper small curve as in step 4, opposite.

3. On the upper edges, mark a distance from the cut curve equal to the desired veil front length plus 1" (2.5 cm) (1). On the fold, mark a distance from the cut curve to the desired veil back length plus 1" (2.5 cm) (2). Fold the upper edge down diagonally to align to the back fold. On the new fold, mark a distance from the cut curve that is halfway between the front and back lengths (3). Fold the open edges back to align to the diagonal fold. On the new diagonal fold, mark a distance from the cut curve that is halfway between the front length and the length to point 3 (4). In line with the new diagonal fold, mark a distance on the lower layers that is halfway between the back length and the length to point 3 (5). Unfold the diagonals. Draw a wide arc connecting the five points.

4. Finish as in step 5, opposite.

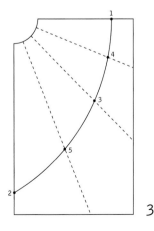

3

FULL-CIRCLE VEIL

A full-circle veil can be attached at the back, perhaps from a bun wrap, Juliet cap, tiara, or comb. Attached at the top of the head, it can be worn with the upper layer as a blusher. Because of the way it is cut, the edges fall in layers of curves, making this style a perfect option for a defining edge finish. Plan for the lower edges of the veil layers to reach two consecutive standard lengths, preferably fingertip and elbow or elbow and shoulder. It may be possible to cut the shorter version from 72" (183 cm) wide illusion; the longer version requires the 108" (274.5 cm) width. Calculate the length needed in step 1 before buying the illusion.

HOW TO MAKE A FULL-CIRCLE VEIL

1. Measure from the point of attachment to the desired length of each layer plus 1" (2.5 cm); add the measurements together. Cut the illusion to this length plus 28" (71 cm).

2. Fold the illusion as in step 2 for the mantilla (page 63). Tie a long string to a pushpin and insert the pin into the work surface at the upper point of the folds. Tie the other end to a fabric marker a distance from the pin equal to the half the total length determined in step 1, above. Draw an arc on the illusion, keeping the marker upright and the string taut between the pushpin and the marker. Cut on the marked line.

3. Unfold illusion. Fold the top of the circle down a distance equal to the desired length of the top layer plus 14½" (36.8 cm). Fold layers in half lengthwise. Retie string to the marker 14" (35.5 cm) from the pushpin. Draw a smaller arc, and cut the illusion.

4. Apply a continuous, reversible edge finish, such as bias binding, pencil edge, or pearl edging to the outer edge of the veil, camouflaging the joint.

5. Fold the upper layer down, aligning the top and bottom edges of the inner circle. Finish the veil as in steps 5 to 7 on page 58, gathering the layers together along the curve.

6. Hang the veil, and shape the edges into even, mirror-image curves; steam gently, if desired, so that on the day of the wedding it can be easily restyled.

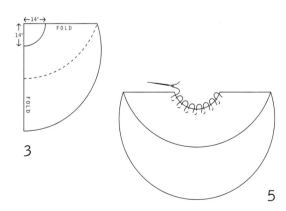

3

5

Poufs

A DIAPHANOUS pouf attached to a headpiece or comb often completes the wedding outfit. Poufs or ruffles can be made in various styles: as hollow, gathered tubes of illusion, multiple bubbles of illusion, or as double ruffles of gathered illusion or other netting. One of the veil edge finishes on pages 72 to 93 can be applied to the open edges of a ruffle pouf to give it more impact.

ABOVE *Made of point d'esprit, this pouf and short veil add interesting texture to an otherwise plain picture hat.*

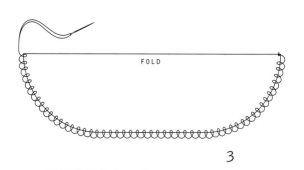

FOLD

3

HOW TO MAKE A TUBE POUF

1. Cut a strip of 72" (183 cm) illusion or a full width of point d'esprit or tulle, 8" to 14" (20.5 to 35.5 cm) wide. (The finished pouf will have a height of slightly less than half the cut width.) Fold the strip in half lengthwise; round the open corners.

2. Thread a needle with double thread, knot the ends together. Secure the thread to one end of the strip at the fold as in step 5 on page 58.

3. Gather the cut edges of the strip together, stitching as shown in step 6, page 58. Pull up on the gathering stitches, gathering the pouf to the desired length; knot the thread. Distribute the gathers evenly along the threads.

4. Hand-stitch the pouf to the back underside edge of a headpiece or to a wide comb or barrette, as on page 70. Separate the layers of the tube to puff them out.

HOW TO MAKE A BUBBLE POUF

1. Cut a strip of 72" (183 cm) illusion, 14" (35.5 cm) wide. Divide the outer edges into five or seven equal spaces; mark both edges.

2. Thread a long needle with double thread, at least 20" (51 cm) long; knot the ends together. Secure the thread to one corner as in the diagram on page 58, step 5. Stitch in the pattern shown in diagram, below, wrapping the stitches around the edges and taking ½" (1.3 cm) running stitches across the strip. Pull up on the threads as necessary, so the entire piece can be gathered at once.

3. Pull up on the gathers to the desired length, creating five or seven bubbles of illusion; distribute the fullness evenly. Knot the thread. Secure the pouf to a headpiece.

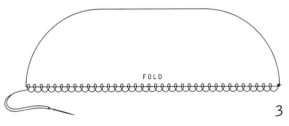

3

HOW TO MAKE A RUFFLE POUF

1. Cut a strip of 72" (183 cm) illusion or a full width of point d'esprit or tulle, 8" to 14" (20.5 to 35.5 cm) wide. (The finished ruffle will have a height of half the cut width.) Fold the strip in half lengthwise; round the open corners.

2. Apply a continuous reversible edge finish (pages 72 to 93) to the outer edges, beginning and ending at the center of one rounded end. Or apply heavy nylon fish line to the outer edge for ruffles that shape into deep curves.

3. Fold the strip in half, lengthwise; press the fold lightly. Secure a double thread to one end of the fold. Gather along the fold, wrapping stitches over the fold.

4. Pull up on the thread, gathering the ruffle to the desired length; knot the thread. Distribute the gathers evenly along the threads.

5. Secure the ruffle to a headpiece, comb, or barrette. Separate the layers of the ruffle.

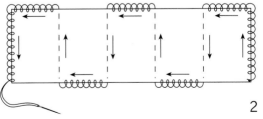

2

Millinery Veiling

FOR the unconventional gal, a classy hat with a small, chic veil may be the crowning touch that distinguishes her as the bride while expressing her unique style. This sophisticated fashion is also a good choice for the second-time bride or for a woman who marries later in life and doesn't feel comfortable in the traditional blushing bride look.

Millinery veils are usually made from more decorative, open nets, like Russian or French veiling, which come in widths of 6" to 18" (15 to 46 cm). The narrower widths are most suited for nose veils on brimless hats; the wider ones can be used for face veils on brimmed hats. The nose veil, so called because it ends just below the tip of the nose, can be attached to the underside of a brimless hat or headpiece, such as the teardrop. A face veil, falling across the face to the chin, can be attached to the top, around the brim of a brimmed hat. If you are making the headpiece, attach the veil before finishing the underside edge in step 4 on page 30. On a brimmed hat, attach the hatband after attaching the veil. There is room for plenty of creativity when making millinery veils; these two methods are a good starting point.

HOW TO MAKE A NOSE VEIL FOR A TEARDROP HAT

1. Cut an 18" (46 cm) piece of net 6" to 9" (15 to 23 cm) wide. Thread a needle with double thread; knot the ends together. Take a stitch through the open mesh at one lower corner; secure the thread by running the needle between the threads before pulling the knot tight.

2. Run gathering stitches up one short side, across the long edge and down the opposite side, wrapping the needle over the edge, in and out of the holes. Pull up on the thread to gather the net in a loose cupped form.

3. Pin the veil to the underside of the teardrop headpiece, with the beginning and end of the gathering at the center sides; pin the veil to the center front underside, also. Distribute the fullness evenly along the outer edge on the underside of the hat; try it on to check the veil placement. Tack in place. If desired, cover the gathered edge of the veil with ribbon or lace, as in step 4 on page 30.

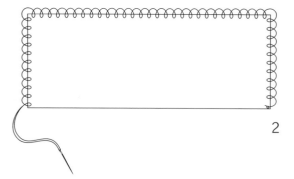

2

HOW TO MAKE A FACE VEIL FOR A BRIMMED HAT

1. Cut a 2 yd. (1.85 m) length of net 18" (46 cm) wide. Stitch the ends together in a ¼" (6 mm) seam, forming a circle.

2. Mark the center front and sides with small safety pins. Gather one long edge, beginning and ending at the back seam.

3. Place the veil over the hat, with the gathered edge encircling the crown and the loose edge hanging over the brim. Pull up on the gathers to fit snugly; align the marks to center front and sides, and distribute the fullness evenly. Hand-tack the veil in place around the base of the crown.

4. Fold the back seam from the bottom up into small pleats; tack to the back crown base.

5. Finish the hat with a hatband; place a bow, pouf, or other embellishments in the back over the pleated seam.

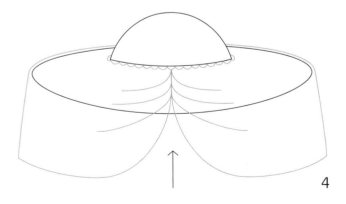

4

THE veil can be attached directly to the headpiece with hand stitches, if the bride will be comfortable wearing it throughout the reception. This is often the choice for veils that are shoulder or elbow length. Alternatively, it can be attached with hook and loop tape and removed after the ceremony, leaving the headpiece in place. Some brides prefer a compromise, stitching a shorter veil or pouf to the headpiece and making a longer underlayer removable for the reception. Making the veil removable, even if you wish to keep it on, may make storage of the headpiece and veil (page 94) a little easier. The methods of attachment differ depending on the veil and headpiece styles.

For a removable veil, create a comfortable, hidden connection with narrow, lightweight, flexible hook and loop tape, available in the bridal department of fabric stores. As a general rule, always position the hook side of the tape away from the hair; if the attachment is on the underside of a headpiece, secure the loop tape to the headpiece and the hook tape to the veil. To prevent the hook tape from snagging the veil after it is removed, cut an extra length of loop tape to cover it.

HOW TO STITCH A VEIL TO A HEADPIECE

Fabric-covered Frame:

1. Tuck the gathered edge of the veil just under the back edge of the headpiece; pin in place. Whipstitch in place by hand to the fabric on the underside of the headpiece. For a horsehair-covered frame, stitch the veil to the wire on the back edge; avoid catching any lace or trim in the stitches.

For a two-tier veil with a pouf, stitch the veil to the lower back edge of the headpiece along the back of the veil gathering line.

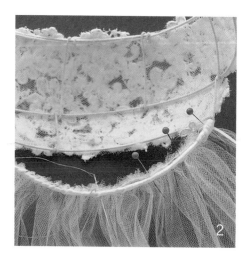

Wire:

1. If the veil will be attached to the wire on the back of a tiara or wreath, wrap the wire with 3/8" (9 mm) wide satin ribbon, wrapping diagonally, and overlapping the edges slightly with each wrap. Secure ribbon ends to the frame with glue.

2. Wrap the upper gathered edge of the veil over the wire, and stitch to the ribbon on the inside edge.

For a two-tier veil with a pouf, stitch the veil to the ribbon on the outside edge, along the veil gathering line.

Comb:

1. Cut a long strip of illusion, 2" (5 cm) wide. Holding one end under your thumb along the top of the comb, wrap the strip around the top of the comb, going once in each space between the teeth; catch the loose end under the first few wraps. Stretch the illusion as you wrap, allowing it to bunch.

2. Trim off excess illusion at the end; tuck the end under the last few wraps. Secure the ends with fabric glue; allow to dry.

3. Wrap the upper edge of the veil over the top of the comb, and hand-stitch it to the illusion heading on the curved underside of the comb.

   For a two-tier veil with a pouf, stitch the veil to the illusion heading on the outside of the comb.

> **TIP** *Removing the veil from a wire leaves it exposed and not particularly attractive. Consider making a pouf or bow to attach to the wire during the reception.*

HOW TO MAKE THE VEIL REMOVABLE

Covered Frame Headpiece:

1. Cut a narrow strip of hook and loop tape the desired width of the upper edge of the veil. Glue the loop side of the strip to the underside of the headpiece, at the desired point of attachment, using fabric glue.

2. Stitch one edge of the hook tape, with the hooks facing up, to the upper edge of the veil. Tuck inside the headpiece and attach to the loop tape.

   For a two-tier veil with a pouf, whipstitch one edge of the hook tape, with the hooks facing up, to the back of the gathering line. Tuck the tape inside the headpiece and attach to the loop tape.

Wire:

1. Wrap the wire with ribbon as in step 1, opposite. Glue a narrow strip of loop tape to the inner edge of the wire.

2. Stitch one edge of the hook tape, with the hooks facing down, to the upper edge of the veil. Wrap over the top of the wire and attach to the loop tape.

Edge Finishes

*W*HETHER subtle or bold, a decorative finish defines the outer edge of your veil, adding a distinct, flowing line to your complete image. The finish may be a very understated, barely visible, fine cord sewn to the outer edge, known as a pencil edge. For a bolder statement, bias binding or lace edging add visual weight to the veil, making it a more prominent part of your overall ensemble. Your other choices include a variety of trims and techniques, each with its own unique appearance that will influence the look of your veil, wed it more closely to your headpiece, and, ultimately, to your complete costume.

Whether or not to edge your veil and the style of edging you select are influenced by several factors. If your dress is very elaborately detailed and you want nothing else to draw attention away from it, perhaps a plain cut edge is best. Without edge definition of any kind, the veil simply becomes a gossamer cloud of illusion. If the dress is more understated, an edge finish on the veil can add style and give the entire outfit more personality. Consider the veil length and at what height the edging will appear, so that it does not distort the view of prominent dress details or compete with other dramatic design lines, such as the neckline, a back opening, or a dropped waistline.

Veil edgings are meant to enhance the dress, by repeating fabric, lace, or an element used for embellishment. Bias silk shantung binding, for example, is the perfect complement for a dress of the same fabric. Narrow satin ribbon or satin rattail edging make perfect fashion sense when paired with a satin gown or might be used to emphasize satin dress details. Pearl or beaded veil edging seems the perfect option when worn with a dress that features pearl or bead encrusted motifs. Likewise, lace details on a dress are complemented by a lace edging, and ruffles or scallop design lines in the dress can be echoed with rippled or scalloped edge finishes on the veil.

Before gathering the veil, apply the desired edge finish in one continuous line per layer, beginning and ending at the top cut edge or fold. For veils with multiple tiers, be sure the edging is applied to the side of each tier that will be facing out. If the veil includes a blusher, use an edge finish that appears reversible. Once the edging has been applied, it may be difficult or impossible to alter the veil length, so be sure to measure and cut accurately.

For many of the techniques, the narrow excess veil edge is trimmed away in the last step, requiring good lighting and the use of a sharp, superior quality scissors. Work over a dark or brightly colored surface so you can see the netting clearly and avoid cutting into your stitches.

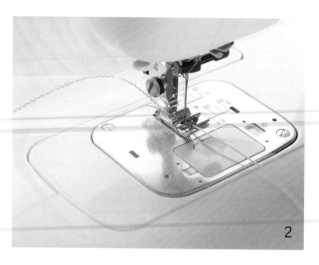

Pencil Edge Finish

A PENCIL edge is very subtle, as if someone took a white pencil and outlined the edge of your veil. It it especially effective for veils with multiple tiers because it separates the layers visually, without weighing them down, and emphasizes the fullness of the illusion. In its simplicity, it does not add a significant design element or draw attention away from the dress in any way.

There are several similar options for the fine cord that is used to edge the veil: #5 pearl cotton, buttonhole twist, rayon embroidery thread, white upholstery thread, or lightweight nylon cording. The technique is the same for any of these materials. A cording foot or embroidery foot with a guide hole is essential for feeding the cord, freeing both hands to control the billowing illusion. Place the cord itself in a jar on the floor or in a

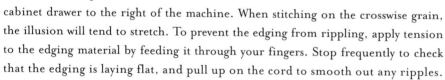

cabinet drawer to the right of the machine. When stitching on the crosswise grain, the illusion will tend to stretch. To prevent the edging from rippling, apply tension to the edging material by feeding it through your fingers. Stop frequently to check that the edging is laying flat, and pull up on the cord to smooth out any ripples.

Another option is to simply serge a tiny rolled hem on the edge of the veil, using only the serger threads to form the edging. Follow the directions in your serger handbook to set up the machine, and test various stitch settings to determine the desired look. If your serger has a differential feed, adjust it slightly higher when stitching on the bias and crosswise grain of the illusion.

Rippled Edge Finish

SIMILAR in method to the pencil edge, the rippled edging is stitched over 20-pound-test fish line. After stitching, the illusion is stretched over the fish line. The resulting curly edge creates a fanciful effect, giving the bridal veil frilly, exuberant character.

HOW TO APPLY A PENCIL EDGE FINISH

1. Thread the machine with fine white thread or monofilament nylon thread in the top and bobbin. (We have used blue thread for clarity.) Set the sewing machine for a narrow zigzag stitch, just wide enough to pass over the cord. Attach a cording foot or an embroidery foot with a hole in the toe for feeding the cord, if available.

2. Position cord ½" (1.3 cm) from the edge of the veil, beginning at the top cut edge or even with the intended fold between tiers. Feed the cord through the guide or hole in the presser foot, pulling a short excess tail of it to the back of the foot. Backstitch to begin, then zigzag over the cord.

3. Overlap ends, if stitching completely around a veil that will be folded into two layers. Or cut cord at the opposite cut edge. Seal ends with a dot of glue or fray preventer. Trim excess illusion close to stitching.

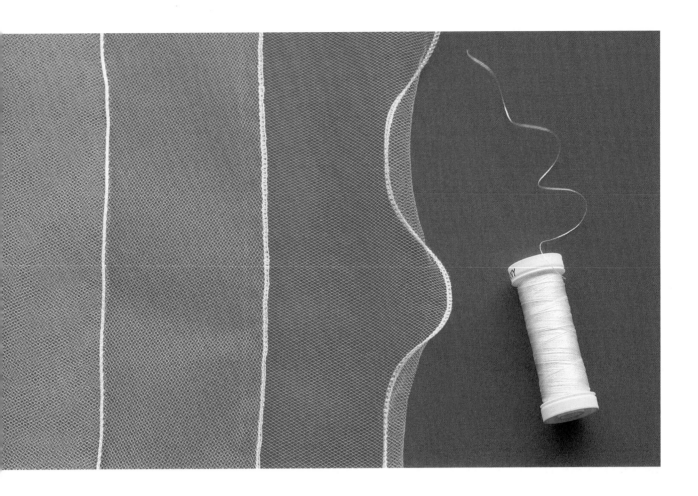

ABOVE (LEFT TO RIGHT) *Corded pencil edge finish, serged edge finish, and rippled edge finish.*

HOW TO APPLY A RIPPLED EDGE FINISH BY CONVENTIONAL MACHINE

1. Follow steps 1 and 2, opposite. Before stitching, knot the fish line to a small button, to prevent it from pulling through the stitches; leave a 1 yd. (0.92 m) tail. Stretch the illusion as you stitch.

2. Remove the veil from the machine, but do not cut the fish line from the reel. Trim the excess illusion close to the stitches.

3. Spread the veil over the fish line, rippling the veil as desired; work from the center toward the ends. Cut the fish line; knot the ends together (if stitched in a complete circle) or to the illusion.

HOW TO APPLY A RIPPLED EDGE FINISH BY SERGER

1. Adjust the serger for a rolled hem stitch; attach a gimp foot, if available. Insert the fish line through the gimp foot (or under the back and over the front of the regular foot); leave a long tail, tied to a button. Stitch over the fish line about 4" (10 cm).

2. Place the veil under the presser foot, over fish line, 1/2" (1.3 cm) from the edge; stitch, trimming the excess veil and keeping the fish line between the needle and knives, if using a regular presser foot.

3. Stitch over fish line 4" (10 cm) at the end; do not cut the fish line from the reel. Finish as in step 3, left.

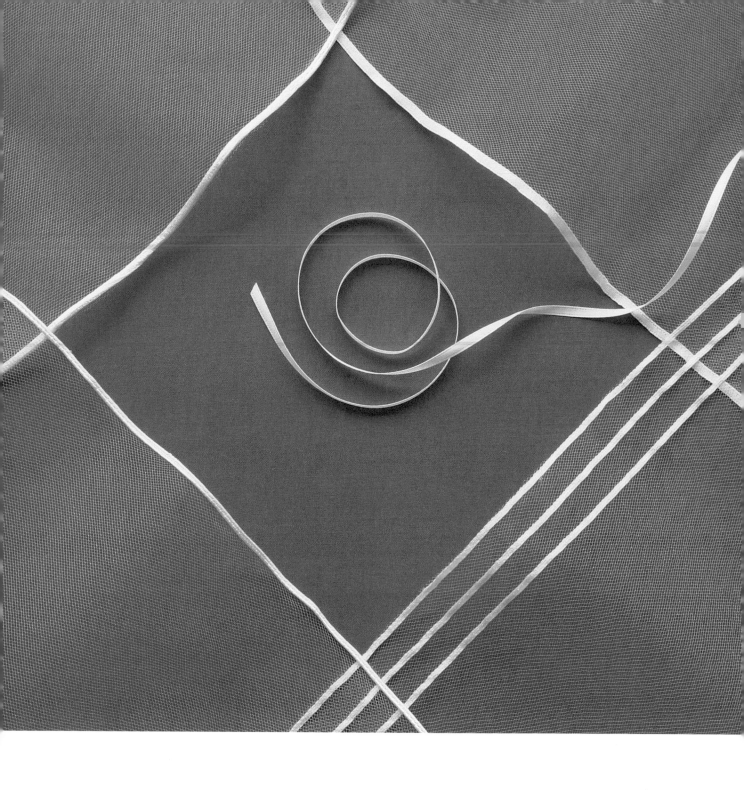

Ribbon, Soutache Braid, or Rattail Edge Finish

OPPOSITE (CLOCKWISE FROM UPPER RIGHT) *Edge finish with* ¹/₈" *(3 mm) satin ribbon, triple ribbon edge with* ¹/₁₆" *(1.5 mm) ribbons, soutache braid edge finish, and rattail edge finish.*

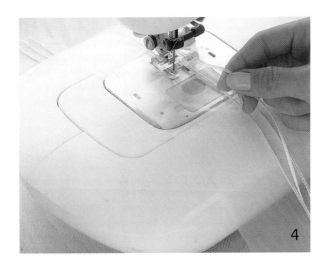

4

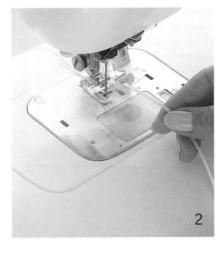

2

SEVERAL trims can be applied to the veil edge using a simple straight stitch. They include narrow ribbon, ¹/₈" or ¹/₁₆" (3 or 1.5 mm) wide, soutache braid, and satin rattail. It is best to purchase these trims in the full length needed from a bolt, rather than in precut packages, if possible, because joins in the trims are hard to disguise. Specially designed presser feet for both conventional machines and sergers are available for feeding the trims with precision, leaving both hands free to guide and control the veil. If your machine is not equipped with one, you can order one that will fit any brand machine from Creative Feet™ (see sources on page 96.) Follow the manufacturer's instructions for attaching and using their presser feet.

> TIP *Both thick and thin rattail can be applied using a zigzag stitch, but the stitches crossing back and forth over the rattail detract from its naturally sleek sheen. Straight stitches are less noticeable, because they tend to sink into the rattail and disappear. The key is to use a fine, sharp needle and fine thread.*

HOW TO APPLY RIBBON, SOUTACHE, OR RATTAIL EDGING

1. Set the machine for a straight stitch of 2.5 mm. Attach a special guide foot, such as the Sequins 'N Ribbon™ foot for ribbon or soutache; attach a cording foot or Pearls 'N Piping™ foot for rattail. Thread the machine with fine thread to match the trim color or monofilament nylon thread in the top and bobbin.

2. Feed the trim through the guide in the specialty presser foot, or place ribbon or soutache ½" (1.3 cm) from the veil edge under an embroidery foot. Stitch the trim to the veil ½" (1.3 cm) from the veil edge. Stitch through the center of ¹/₁₆" (1.5 mm) ribbon, soutache, or rattail, or stitch along one edge of ¹/₈" (3 mm) ribbon. To prevent the edging from rippling when stitching on the bias and crosswise grain, apply tension to the trim by feeding it through your fingers.

3. Trim the excess veil close to the stitching.

4. Stitch additional rows of trim, if desired, using the edge of the presser foot, the throat plate seam guide, or a piece of tape on the machine bed as a guide for distance between rows.

Pearl or Bead Edge Finish

DAINTY molded plastic pearls, available by the yard, or light-catching, cross-locked glass beads, can easily be applied to the veil edge using either a conventional sewing machine or a serger. Special presser feet feed the continuous string, leaving hands free to guide the veil. For applying the pearls using a conventional machine, use a Pearls 'N Piping™ foot. For applying by serger, use a beading foot. Alternatively, individual pearl drops can be sewn by hand to the veil edge at evenly spaced intervals

A pearl veil edge finish is especially fitting when the gown has other pearl features or when bands of shiny satin accent a matte-finish fabric. A coordinating headpiece could also be decorated in some way with pearls. Clear glass beads can be used to play up a shimmery gown fabric or echo beaded, sequined embellishments. This edging could work very well with a metal rhinestone or crystal beaded tiara.

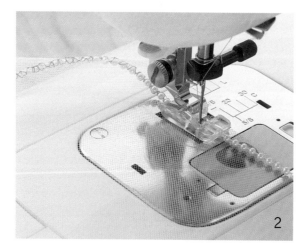

HOW TO APPLY A PEARL EDGE FINISH BY CONVENTIONAL MACHINE

1. Set the machine for a zigzag stitch with a 3 mm to 5 mm width, depending on the size of the pearls, and a stitch length of 2 mm to 2.5 mm. Attach a Pearls 'N Piping foot. Thread the machine with fine white or monofilament nylon thread in the top and bobbin; use a size #70 needle.

2. Feed the pearl strand through the groove in the presser foot. Stitch the strand to the veil ½" (1.3 cm) from the edge. Trim off the excess veil.

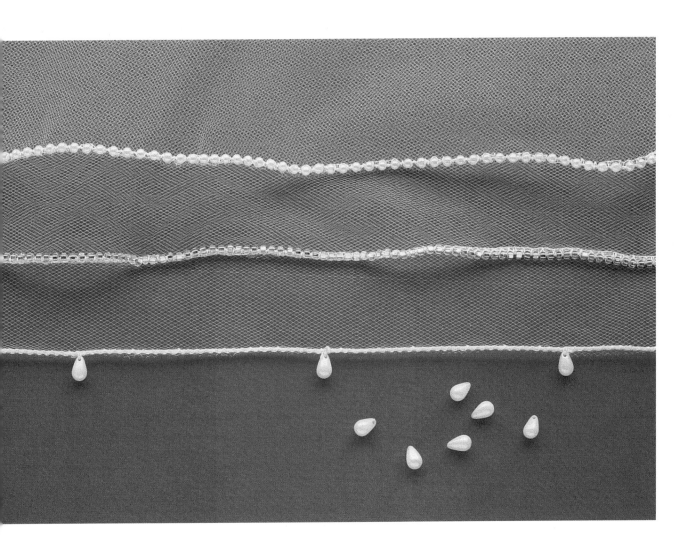

HOW TO APPLY A PEARL EDGE FINISH BY SERGER

1. Set the serger for a rolled hem; attach a beading foot. Use monofilament nylon thread in the right or left needle and loopers. Adjust the stitch length to match the pearl size.

2. Guiding the pearls in the groove of the foot, stitch ½" (1.3 cm) from the edge, trimming excess veil and locking the pearls to the edge in one step. If your serger has differential feed, adjust it slightly higher when stitching on the crosswise grain of the illusion to prevent the edge from rippling. (Test to determine exact setting.)

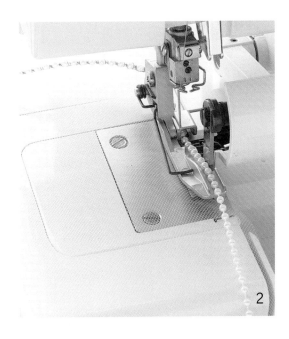

ABOVE (TOP TO BOTTOM)
Continuous pearl edge finish, cross-locked bead edge finish, and single pearl drops hand-stitched along a pencil edge finish.

Lace Edge Finishes

A DELICATE, narrow lace edge finish can be used to emphasize the flowing lines of a single or multiple-tier veil. This treatment is naturally suitable when worn with a gown that also has lace, perhaps at the hem or bodice or scattered motifs on the skirt. For continuity, you should use the same kind of lace (page 10) for the edge finish as is found on the gown and headpiece, though it need not be a matching pattern. Narrow lace edgings have one straight edge and one decorative edge, in widths that range from 1/4" to 6" (6 mm to 15 cm); of course the wider

HOW TO APPLY A NARROW LACE EDGING

1. Plan the placement of dominant lace motifs so that they will fall directly across from each other on each side of the face. Overlap the lace edge onto the illusion 1/2" (1.3 cm); pin in place, if necessary.

2. Secure the lace to the veil, using a straight stitch or narrow zigzag along the inner edge.

3. Trim away excess veil close to the stitches.

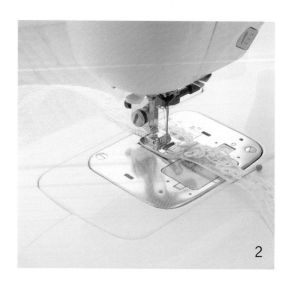

2

1. Determine the placement of the lace on the veil. Pin the lace to the veil, starting at the center front and working toward the center back. Clip the lace between motifs and overlap the pieces as necessary to lay flat around curves.

2. Arrange additional lace appliqués or small motifs at center front and back to disguise joints, if necessary, or to create interesting focal points, if desired. Hand-stitch individual motifs in place.

3. Stitch the lace to the veil, using short straight stitches or zigzag stitches along the inner edge of the lace.

4. Trim illusion from behind the lace, about 1/8" (3 mm) from the stitching.

the lace, the more weight it will add to the veil edge and the more difficult it will be to shape around curves. Avoid lace edgings that have a definite one-way design. You will be unable to reverse the lace, so it will be running up on one side of the veil and down on the other. Galloon laces are decorative on both edges and also come in a range of styles and widths. They can be cut apart down the middle to create two narrow strips.

Wide lace creates a very bold edge finish for a single-layer veil and is a classic edge trim for a mantilla. Alençon and Venice laces can be cut apart between motifs and overlapped to ease around curves. Individual motifs may also be cut from Alençon lace fabric and sewn separately around the outer edge of the veil. If continuous lace has a strong one-way pattern, you want the direction to be running up, toward the face on both sides, aligning motifs horizontally. The joints at the center front and back are disguised by artfully arranging lace elements to form a focal point.

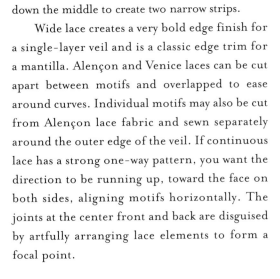

Bias Bound Edge Finish

VEIL edges encased in bias binding offer a bold, tailored look. For best results, the binding should be a very lightweight natural-fiber fabric, like silk shantung, which will hold a pressed edge and easily conform to curves. Bound edges can be from ¼" to 1½" (6 mm to 3.8 cm) wide. The wider the binding, the bolder the look and the more dominant will be the role of the veil in the total ensemble.

To estimate the number of yards (meters) of bias strip needed, add the lengths of the sides and bottom edges of each veil tier and divide by 36" (91.5 cm). Consult the chart at right for an estimate of the length of bias strip a square of fabric will yield.

BIAS STRIP YIELDS FROM 44" (112 cm) SQUARE

Finished Width	Cut Width	Yield
¼" (6 mm)	1" (2.5 cm)	54 yd. (49.7 m)
½" (1.3 cm)	2" (5 cm)	27 yd. (24.8 m)
¾" (2 cm)	3" (7.5 cm)	18 yd. (16.5 m)
1" (2.5 cm)	4" (10 cm)	13 yd. (11.9 m)
1¼" (3.2 cm)	5" (12.7 cm)	10¾ yd. (9.9 m)
1½" (3.8 cm)	6" (15 cm)	9 yd. (8.28 m)

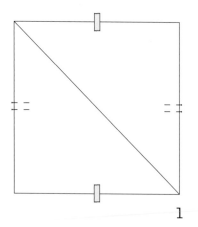

1

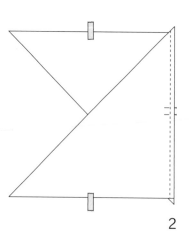

2

HOW TO MAKE CONTINUOUS BIAS BINDING

1. Cut a 44" (112 cm) square of fabric; trim off the selvages. Mark the upper and lower edges of the square with tape; mark the left and right edges with pins. Cut diagonally from the top left corner to the bottom right corner.

2. Flip the left triangle over vertically onto the right triangle, right sides together, aligning pin-marked edges; pin and stitch together, using ¼" (6 mm) seam allowances. Press the seam open.
(Continued)

ABOVE *Silk shantung bias bound edge finishes in two different widths.*

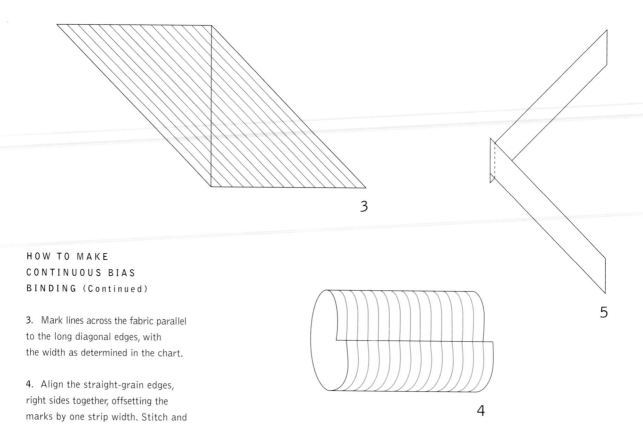

3

4

5

HOW TO MAKE
CONTINUOUS BIAS
BINDING (Continued)

3. Mark lines across the fabric parallel
to the long diagonal edges, with
the width as determined in the chart.

4. Align the straight-grain edges,
right sides together, offsetting the
marks by one strip width. Stitch and
press the seam open. Cut around the
tube on the marked lines, cutting
one continuous bias strip. Wrap the
bias strip loosely onto cardboard
for easy use.

5. To attach two continuous bias
strips, place the ends of the strips,
right sides together, at a right angle;
stitch on the lengthwise grain,
as shown. Trim the seam to ¼"
(6 mm); press open.

6. Feed the bias strip into a bias
tape maker, using a pin to get
it started. The strip will fold into
binding as it is pulled though the tool;
press the folds in place. With the
iron resting on the binding, gently
slide the bias tape maker down
the length of the strip; press, but do
not stretch the binding.

7. Press the binding in half lengthwise, encasing the folds. Align the
folds exactly if you intend to stitch
one side and glue the other; offset
one edge slightly if you intend to
stitch both sides. Wrap the binding
back onto the cardboard for
easier handling.

6

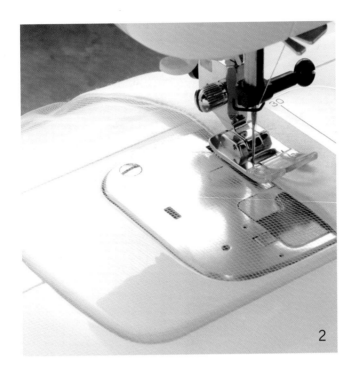

2

HOW TO APPLY
BINDING BY SEWING

1. Press-shape the binding to fit the veil edge without puckering, with the shorter fold on the right side. Align the raw edge of the short side to the raw edge of the veil, right sides together. Stitch in the well of the fold.

2. Fold the wider side of the binding over the veil edge to the wrong side. Stitch in the ditch from the right side, catching the binding on the back of the veil.

HOW TO APPLY BINDING
BY SEWING AND GLUING

1. Press-shape the binding to fit the veil edge without puckering. Align the raw edge of the binding to the edge of the veil, right sides together. Stitch in the well of the fold.

2. Fold the binding over the edge of the veil to the wrong side, aligning the top and bottom folds. Dilute flexible fabric glue to a spreading consistency. Working in small sections, slip paper towel under the raw edge of the binding; lightly brush glue onto the binding. Reposition, and finger-press in place.

Scalloped Edge Finishes

THE EDGES of your veil can be shaped into soft scallops in several techniques that vary in their degree of emphasis. Simply cutting the veil's outer edge into deep scallops softens the look and adds interest without adding more design lines. For a more pronounced effect, the deep scallops can be satin-stitched or edged with a fine cord (page 74), soutache braid, or rattail (page 76). This can be very effective on a ballet or chapel length veil.

On a smaller scale, many sewing machines have built-in scallop stitch patterns, either as straight stitches or satin stitches, and the length and depth of the scallops can be adjusted. The density of the stitches and the closeness of the scallops affect the overall appearance of the veil. The resulting frilly look is more emphatic on a multi-layered or very full veil.

For any of the stitched methods, strips of stabilizer placed under the illusion keep the edge from being distorted and offer support for the stitches. The remaining stabilizer is easily torn and rinsed away, leaving a smooth, patterned edge.

BELOW (LEFT TO RIGHT) *Small machine-programmed satin-stitch scallops, machine-programmed straight-stitch scallops, large hand-guided satin-stitch scallops, and plain scallop-cut edge finish.*

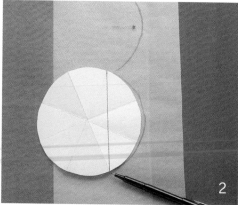

HOW TO SCALLOP-CUT A VEIL EDGE

1. Cut out a 5" or 6" (12.7 or 15 cm) paper circle. Fold the circle in half three times, dividing it into eighths; open out the circle. Draw a straight line connecting points on the circle that are three-eighths apart.

2. Fold the veil in half lengthwise and pin it together within 3" (7.5 cm) of the outer edge. Beginning at the upper edge and using a fine-point permanent marker, mark scallops along the veil edge. Align the center of each scallop to the cut edge of the veil, and trace the marked arc of the circle for each scallop, keeping the straight line parallel to the veil edge. When going around curves, keep both end points the same distance from the outer edge.

3. Stop marking within 18" (46 cm) of the center bottom. Mark a half scallop at the center fold, and measure the remaining distance. Finish marking, adjusting the size of each scallop slightly to fit the space.

4. Cut the scallops, trimming away the marked lines and cutting both layers at once. Take care not to overcut the corners.

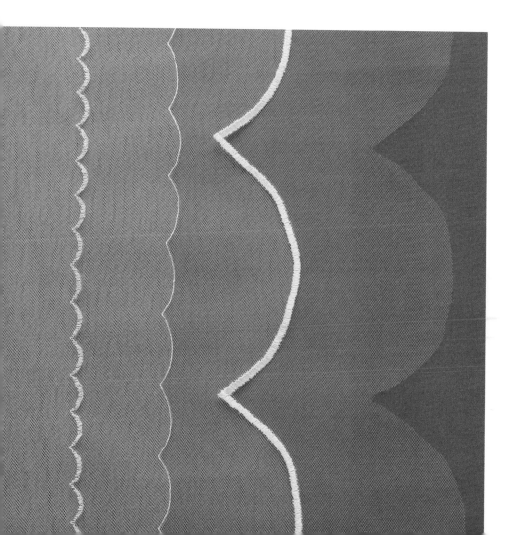

HOW TO STITCH
SMALL-SCALE SCALLOPS

1. Set the sewing machine for a decorative scallop stitch, following your owner's manual. Attach an embroidery foot. Thread the machine with rayon embroidery thread in the top and bobbin for a lustrous finish or with cotton embroidery thread for a matte finish.

2. Cut water-soluble stabilizer into 1" (2.5 cm) strips. Place a strip under the veil edge. Stitch the scallops about ½" (1.3 cm) from the outer edge, feeding the stabilizer strips under the illusion as you go along; use shorter stabilizer strips along curves.

3. Tear away excess stabilizer gently. Trim away excess illusion close to stitches. Rinse veil edge in cool water to remove any remaining stabilizer; allow to air dry. Press lightly with a warm iron, using a press cloth.

HOW TO SATIN-STITCH
LARGE SCALLOPS

1. Follow steps 1 to 3, opposite, making sure marks transfer to lower layer of illusion; remove pins and unfold veil. Cut lightweight tear-away stabilizer into strips slightly wider than the scallop depth; pin strips in place under marked scallops.

2. Set the sewing machine for a wide satin stitch. Attach an embroidery foot. Thread the machine with rayon embroidery thread in the top and bobbin for a lustrous finish or with cotton embroidery thread for a matte finish.

3. Stitch just inside the marked line; stop and pivot the presser foot at each inner corner.

4. Tear away excess stabilizer gently. Trim away excess illusion close to stitches.

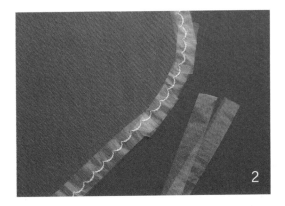

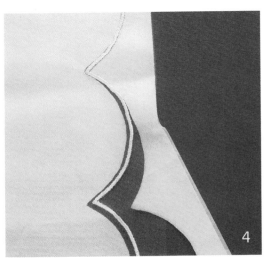

HOW TO APPLY A NARROW EDGE
FINISH TO A SCALLOPED EDGE

Follow step 1, for large satin-stitched scallops. Then follow the directions for the specific trim (page 74 or 76). At each corner, leave the needle down in the fabric, raise the presser foot, and pivot to continue. Finish, following step 4 for large satin-stitched scallops.

Passementerie

SOUTACHE braid and thin rattail can be manipulated into curves, loops, and swirls to create strong design detail along the veil edge. Because this technique, known as passementerie, adds both visual and real weight to the veil, it is recommended for single layer veils with less fullness, including mantilla styles. A veil with soutache passementerie might be worn with a gown that features Alençon lace, as the soutache resembles the cord used to accent the floral motifs in the lace. Rattail passementerie, trimming the outer edges of a long veil, works well with a simple or more tailored satin gown, allowing the veil to become the focal point.

Typically, the passementerie design will meander in gently waving lines between evenly spaced clusters of loops that resemble flower petals, hearts, or bows. Plan the clusters to fall at levels where you would invite attention, such as at the shoulders, waistline, and fingertips; points that just happen to be even distances apart.

It is difficult to stitch across and turn tight loops with rattail. It can be done successfully, though, using a combination of stitching and gluing. Stitching across soutache, because of its lower profile, can be done easily, though turning the frothy mounds of illusion repeatedly to form loops and curves can be a challenge. Stitching evenly and neatly on the easily distorted netting takes patience and the use of a stabilizer. Though slightly more tedious than some of the other edge finishes, the results are very dramatic.

HOW TO APPLY SOUTACHE PASSEMENTERIE

1. Draw the desired pattern on paper; design it to fit the veil curves. Cut strips of water-soluble stabilizer wide enough to accommodate the pattern; baste them to the right and wrong sides of the veil edge. Trace the pattern on the stabilizer, using water-soluble or disappearing ink marker.

2. Set the machine for a 1.5 to 2 mm straight stitch. Insert a sharp size #70 needle. Thread the machine with fine white or monofilament nylon thread in the top and bobbin. Attach a cording foot; run the soutache braid through the hole in the cording foot.

3. Stitch at a slow, even pace over the design lines, turning the veil as necessary. Keep the illusion and stabilizer flat so the pattern is not distorted.

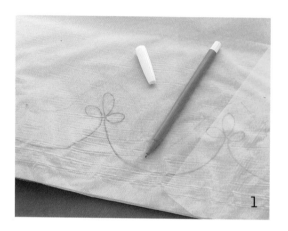

4. Gently tear away the stabilizer; remove any remaining stabilizer by rinsing with cold water. Press lightly with warm iron and press cloth.

5. Trim away the veil edge, if desired, cutting close to the outer edge of the braid.

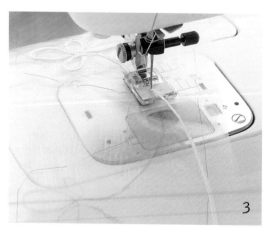

TIP In place of a cording foot, put a piece of plastic tape across the toes of an open-toe embroidery foot; puncture with the machine needle. Widen the hole slightly to accept the soutache, and thread the braid through the hole.

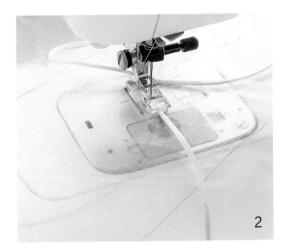

2

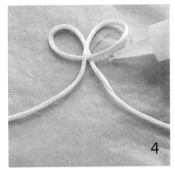

4

BELOW *Soutache and rattail passementerie edge finishes.*

HOW TO APPLY RATTAIL PASSEMENTERIE

1. Follow steps 1 to 3, opposite, feeding thin rattail under the groove of a Pearls 'N Piping™ foot.

2. When you reach an area of the design with loops, stitch several times in place to lock the threads. Raise the presser foot and draw enough rattail through to the back of the foot to cover the design lines in the looped area. Move the presser foot to a point just beyond the looped area, and stitch in place several times to lock the threads as you begin stitching again.

3. Repeat step 2 around the veil to complete the design. Remove the stabilizer. Place the pattern on the work surface; cover the unfinished area of the design with a sheet of wax paper. Place the veil over the pattern matching up the finished areas to the pattern.

4. Trace the loops with a thin line of fabric glue; press the rattail in place. Allow to dry.

5. Repeat steps 3 and 4 at each unfinished area of the design. Trim away the veil edge, if desired, cutting close to the outer edge of the rattail.

Thread Sketch Embroidery

DELICATELY embroidered thread sketches that resemble Schiffli lace can be stitched onto your veil, adding an elegant dimension. Individual embroidery motifs, evenly arranged toward the outer and lower edges, can accompany a scalloped or pencil edge finish. Or a meandering design, such as a vine with leaves, can become an edge finish in itself. This technique can be used to imitate a lace design on the gown or simply to add a little texture and interest to an ensemble with little or no decoration. Look for inspiration in design books, stencils, embroidery patterns, or laces, and modify the designs to suit the technique and your taste.

OPPOSITE *A freehand machine*
embroidered sketch can be designed
to resemble lace used in the gown.

HOW TO APPLY THREAD SKETCH EMBROIDERY

1. Set the machine for a straight stitch; adjust the stitch length to 0. Cover or lower the feed dogs and remove the presser foot; attach a darning foot, if desired. Insert a sharp #70 needle. Thread the machine with rayon embroidery thread for a lustrous appearance or with cotton embroidery thread for a matte appearance.

2. Transfer the design to water-soluble stabilizer. Place the stabilizer over the veil in the desired position; place another layer of stabilizer underneath. Place the layers over the outer ring of an embroidery hoop; insert the inner ring from the top. Place the hoop under the needle; lower the presser foot lever to engage the upper thread tension.

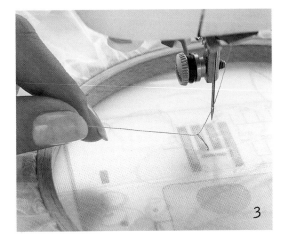

3. Rotate the handwheel, while holding the needle thread, to bring the bobbin thread to the top of the work. Stitch several stitches in one spot to anchor threads. Clip thread tails.

4. Hold the hoop flat against the machine bed with both hands. Run the machine at a steady pace, and trace the outline of the design, using the needle as a pencil; keep the hoop facing in one direction. Stitch over design lines two or three times for more definition.

5. Fill in open areas of the design with parallel wavy lines, crosshatching patterns, or echo lines for more density. Stitch several stitches in one spot to anchor thread; clip.

6. Reposition the embroidery hoop as necessary to complete the sketch around the veil edge. Carefully tear away as much of the stabilizer as possible. Trim away veil edge close to stitches, if design is intended to be an edge finish. Dip the design in cold water to remove any traces of stabilizer and marking pen. Rinse again with fresh water. Allow to dry; press with warm iron and press cloth.

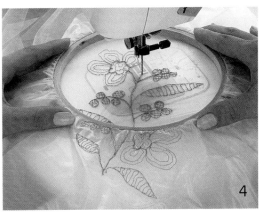

TIP *Machine embroidered designs that begin at the cheekbone and end just above the collarbone are very flattering to the bride.*

Scattered Embellishments

3

GIVE the veil more prominence by scattering lace motifs, pearl clusters, beads and sequins, or tiny ribbon roses over the illusion. Gluing is the preferred method for securing the embellishments to the veil, and it is easiest to do it with the illusion spread out flat before gathering. Concentrate the embellishments toward the outer edge, in small clusters, or spread them out evenly over the entire veil. Keep in mind that items spaced evenly when the illusion is flat will be more concentrated near the head after the veil is gathered.

HOW TO APPLY LACE MOTIF EMBELLISHMENTS

1. Cut individual lace motifs from Alençon or Venice lace fabric or trim; seal any cut edges that are apt to ravel, using liquid fray preventer. Or purchase lace appliqués in mirror-image pairs.

2. Pin the lace motifs to the right side of the illusion in the desired positions. Place the illusion, right side down, on a protected surface.

3. Dip a sponge pouncer (used for stencil painting) in a puddle of clear fabric glue; blot off excess. Dab the pouncer evenly over each motif; glue will pass through the illusion and onto the lace back. Allow to dry; remove pins.

> TIP *Before you do any gluing, pin motifs in place. Gather up the veil in your hand and look at the finished effect in a mirror.*

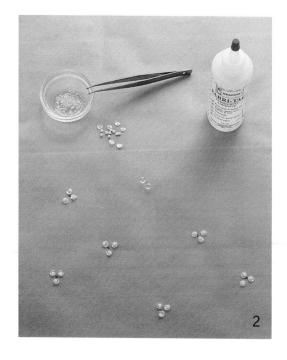

2

HOW TO APPLY SCATTERED PEARLS, BEADS, OR SEQUINS

1. Determine the desired placement pattern; mark a large sheet of paper as a guide. Spread the illusion, face-up, over the guide, working in one area at a time.

2. Pick up individual pearls, beads, or sequins with a tweezers; dip in clear glue and place on illusion. Cluster three items at each location for more effect. Glue beads to the center of sequins. Allow to dry before moving to another area.

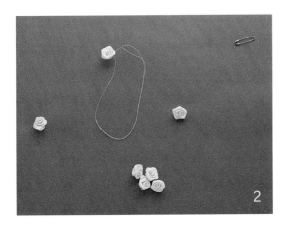

HOW TO APPLY RIBBON ROSES

1. Determine the desired placement pattern; mark the illusion with small safety pins. Gather veil in hand to check placement.

2. Hand-tack each ribbon rose in place, using needle and thread; cross several filaments of the netting with each stitch, for secure attachment.

BELOW (CLOCKWISE FROM LEFT) *Clustered pearls over sequins, scattered lace appliqués, and hand-stitched ribbon roses.*

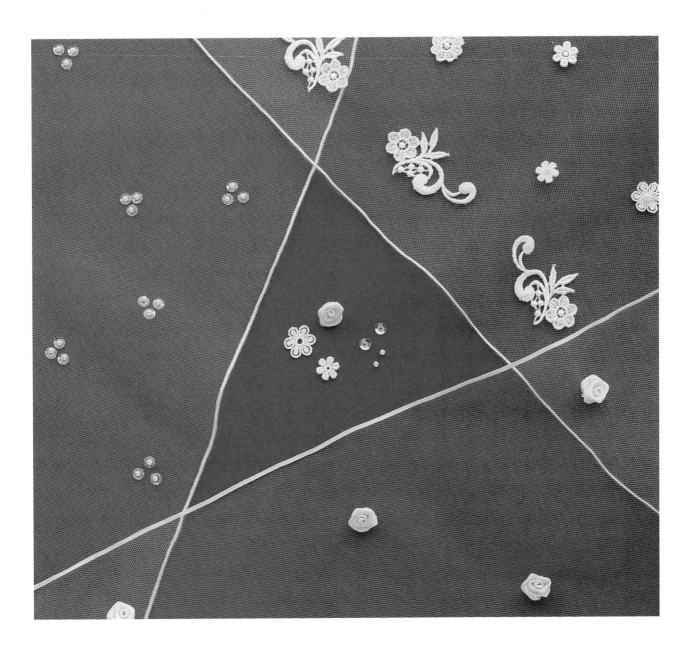

Care & Storage of the Headpiece & Veil

YOUR headpiece and veil are a part of your family heritage, especially if they were handmade by you or someone close to you. It is conceivable that one day in the future, someone you love may ask for the honor of wearing your headpiece and veil for her wedding. Even if they are never worn by another bride, it is important to store them with great care.

If you plan to remove the veil for the reception, bring a large pillowcase with you for temporary storage. Roll the veil gently and tuck it away inside the pillowcase. It is not necessary to dry clean the headpiece and veil; in fact dry cleaning could damage them. Inspect the headpiece for missing pearls or loose lace, and do any minor repair work that is necessary.

Place the headpiece and veil in a non-buffered, acid-free box, apart from the wedding dress. If the veil is detachable, store it in a separate box from the headpiece. Build a support for the headpiece by wrapping crumpled acid-free tissue paper around a Styrofoam® ball. Wrap the headpiece with acid-free tissue paper, and place it over the support. Stuff more of the tissue paper around it in the box, to keep it from shifting. Tuck sheets of acid-free tissue paper between the layers of the veil; fold it gently, and wrap it with a clean cotton sheet or pillowcase, not plastic. Over time, the fumes from plastic will discolor fabrics, glues, and trims. Toss in a few packets of desiccant to protect against humidity.

Store the boxes in a dark, dry place, such as a closet or under a bed. Avoid attics, where temperature extremes can damage your precious treasures; avoid basements, where mildew and tiny critters can invade. Shield boxes from dust with old sheets. Avoid plastic wraps that can cause condensation to form.

Non-buffered, acid free tissue paper, desiccants, and storage boxes are available from bridal shops or from stores that specialize in archival materials.

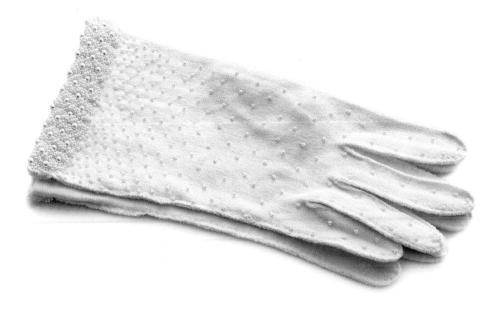

SOURCES

GLUES & ADHESIVES

Beacon Adhesives
125 MacQuesten Parkway S.
Mount Vernon, NY 10550
www.beaconadhesives.com
(800) 865-7238

Duncan Enterprises
5673 E. Shields Ave.
Fresno, CA 93727
www.duncancrafts.com
(800) 438-6226

MILLINERY SUPPLIES

Judith M Hat
   & Millinery Supplies
104 S. Detroit St.
LaGrange, IN 46761-1806
www.judithm.com
(877) 499-4407

Milliners Supply Company
911 Elm St.
Dallas, TX 75202
www.milliners.com
(800) 6-BRIDES

RIBBON

C.M. Offray & Sons, Inc.
Route 24, Box 601
Chester, NJ 07930-0601
www.offray.com
(908) 879-4700

SPECIALTY PRESSER FEET

Creative Feet
8933 E. Laredo Dr.
Prescott Valley, AZ 86314
www.sewingmachinefeet.com
(800) 776-6938

STORAGE

University Products
517 Main St., P.O. Box 101
Holyoke, MA 01040-0101
www.universityproducts.com
(800) 628-1912

INDEX